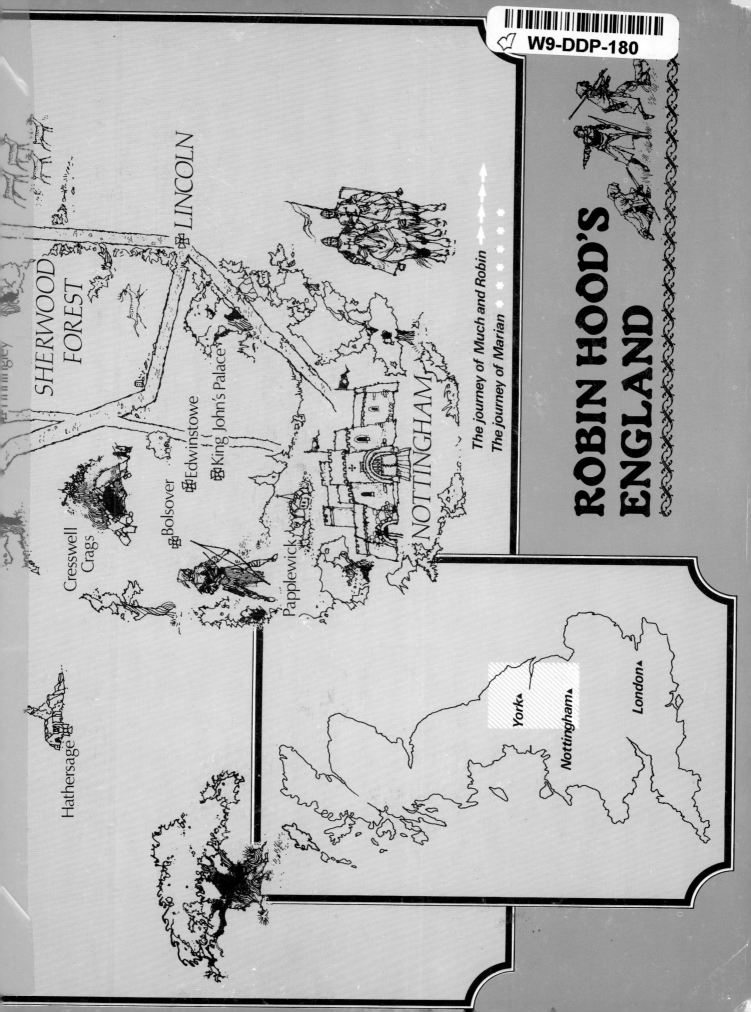

SHERWOOD FOREST

LINCOLN

Cresswell Crags

Bolsover

Edwinstowe

King John's Palace

Papplewick

NOTTINGHAM

Hathersage

The journey of Much and Robin
The journey of Marian

ROBIN HOOD'S ENGLAND

York

Nottingham

London

Robin Hood
His Life and Legend

Bernard Miles

Illustrated by
Victor G. Ambrus

RAND McNALLY & COMPANY
Chicago · New York · San Francisco

Contents

© Copyright 1979 by
The Hamlyn Publishing Group Limited
London · New York · Sydney · Toronto
This edition published 1979 by
Rand McNally & Company
Chicago · New York · San Francisco

ISBN 528-82340-X

Library of Congress Catalog Card No. 79.64615
Printed and bound in Spain by Graficromo, S.A. – Cordoba

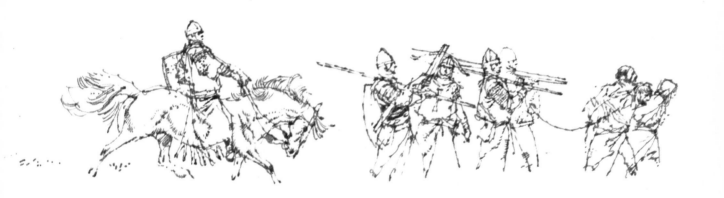

Introduction

When I set out to write this story, I thought Robin Hood was a kind of fairytale figure. But when I went to some of the many places named after him, especially those in north Yorkshire, I began to see him as a true historical character, just as solid as some of the great heroes of the American West. Indeed, in many of the ancient places I visited I had the feeling that I was actually in his presence. Of course my friends laughed at me. They said the Robin Hood story was only a myth. To this I replied that myth is all too often history raised to a higher level, lifted into the realm of poetry.

So I have treated Robin's adventures as a true story, but one so popular that, like many other good stories, it got varied and added to over the centuries. Fresh characters were fitted in, fresh dangers invented, fiercer battles, more daring escapes. For Robin represented to the poor, uneducated people of those far-off days what King Arthur and his Knights represented to the rich and powerful.

Then I found that I actually had some very early ballads in a little green book called *Robin Hood, A Collection of Poems, Songs and Ballads*, collected by a man named John Matthew Gutch in 1866. This contained forty-odd poems about Robin's adventures, the oldest one first published nearly six hundred years ago. It had doubtless been made up a hundred or more years earlier still, then passed from family to family and village to village by word of mouth until printing was invented and it was made into a book.

Out of the dozens of places named after Robin or mentioned in those early poems, I have used the names of many real villages and abbeys, of churches and castles and dungeons and caves. And these places you will find marked on the map inside the covers of the book, so that if ever you get to England you can go on a Robin Hood Holiday, visiting Robin's old haunts and gathering plenty of other history on the way – Stone Age, Bronze Age, Iron Age, Roman, Saxon, Danish, Norman and Tudor, right up to our own times, using Robin as a sort of key to unlock the past that happened before him and the past that has happened since he died – learning history and geography in a new way, not in the classroom, but out in the fields and hills and villages and cities of England.

In Sherwood itself you can see the Major Oak under which Robin and his Men used to gather, and not far away a fine museum which shows how people lived in those early times. In Nottingham you can visit the caves and dungeons underneath the Castle, including the dreaded Mortimer's Hole, where the sheriffs kept their prisoners. And not far away the churches of Edwinstowe and Papplewick where both Robin and Alan a' Dale were married.

In and around Hathersage in the county of Derbyshire you can find many places connected with Little John, including his grave. Further north in York you can visit St. Mary's Abbey, and Pateley Bridge where Friar Tuck was born and Fountains Abbey where he trained to be a monk. Further north still you can find Gisburn and its forest, and Robin Hood's Bay and Mickleby where Much the Miller came from and the beautiful crypt at Lastingham where he and Robin hid, and Hartoft End where Robin lived with Mark and Marian; and all the wonderful castles and abbeys and standing stones in which the north of England is so rich.

In Nottingham itself, in the City Library, they have over seven hundred books devoted to this great story. There you can do your own search for the names of all the places in England that bear Robin's name, and mark them in your own private Robin Hood map.

Finally I must acknowledge help received from a number of friends and well-wishers who lent a generous hand in my quest, including Jack Lindsay, Keith Train, Rogan Jenkinson, Jean Henson, Alan McCormick, June Irvin, David Stagg and Rosalind Carreck. Also from Jan Sutton, Sheila Tobin and Clare Welch who toiled uncomplainingly at their typewriters. And I was very lucky to have Victor Ambrus to bring my story to life with such wonderful illustrations.

To Jack Sprat who took such a lively interest in both text and illustrations.

CHAPTER ONE

Outlawed!

IT was a cold frosty night, with clouds scudding across the moon. Robin quietly opened the door of his hut and stepped out into the shadows with Tricket at his heels. Latching the door behind him, he stood for a few moments, listening. There was no sound except for the north-east wind brushing the trees. So, knotting the lead on to Tricket's collar, he whispered, 'Good girl, quiet now!' and set off into the forest.

Tricket was a young bitch, the last of a litter, just over a year old. When she was born she had been so small and weak that Robin's master had wanted to throw her out into the forest and leave her to die. But she had such beautiful brown eyes and she licked people's hands so lovingly that Robin had begged to keep her. He promised he would teach her to stay inside the walls and hedges of the farm and never to go chasing deer, so his master agreed, and Robin was now training her to walk obediently at his heels and never to dart off when she heard a hare lolloping through the undergrowth or a woodcock clucking on its nest. They usually went out at night when the gamekeepers were fast asleep, or drinking together in their hut.

Once clear of the village Robin unknotted the leash and set Tricket free. Soon they had left Hartoft behind and were deep in the forest. Sometimes they would come to an open glade, then they would dive into the thicket again. They moved swiftly and silently and, even when the trees and bushes were packed tightly together, seemed to find their way through them quite easily.

Suddenly it happened. There was a stir in one of the huge oak trees that towered above their heads. Robin stopped and drew back, but he was too late. A great fisherman's net, weighed down at the edges with heavy stones, dropped from the branches above, completely covering both him and his dog and entangling them in its meshes. They struggled to free themselves, but it was useless. They were caught.

Then two dark figures stepped out from the shadows and two others scrambled down from above. This was a trap laid by the gamekeepers, or foresters as they were called in those days.

'So,' said the one who appeared to be their leader, 'poaching our master's deer!'

'Never!' said Robin. 'I carry no bow and my hound has been trained never to stray from my heels.'

'You must tell that tale in Court,' said the Chief Forester. 'Aye, and prove it,' said one of the others. 'Perhaps the judge will believe you. But 'tis more likely he will believe us.'

Then they lifted the net from the two captives and began to roll it up.

'The dog must stay in pound until the trial,' said the Chief Forester. 'And you must present yourself at the next Forest

Court.' So Robin had to give up the leash and Tricket was taken away and put into a dirty kennel ready to be brought to trial in ten days' time.

The Court was held in one of the farmer's barns and the judge was the Chief of all the Northern Foresters. He sat on a bench and wore a dark red robe and a special hat and he had a clerk to write down all that happened. Tricket was held on her leash by one of the foresters who had laid the trap, and two of the others held Robin firmly by the arms. Tricket whined when she saw Robin but the forester who held her slapped her across the nose and told her to be quiet.

Standing at the back of the Court, amongst the people who had come to see how things would turn out, was a fourteen-year-old boy named Mark and his twin sister Marian. They were children of the farmer for whom Robin worked and on whose farm he lived.

The judge heard Robin's story and then the foresters told theirs. What they said was all lies, but it was four voices against one so Robin had no chance. At last the judge said he was sure that Robin and Tricket had been poaching and that as a punishment Tricket must have one of her paws chopped off so that she would never go poaching again. And this he said must be done at once so that all the village could see.

So a block was brought in and the forester who was holding Tricket led her towards it, laying her right paw in the middle. Tricket whined and Robin struggled to get free, but it was no use. Another forester stepped forward and laid the great chisel on her paw, then raised his hammer ready to strike: and that was the moment that Mark and Marian saved Tricket from her cruel fate, for they suddenly shrieked, 'No, no, no!' And it was their shriek that made the forester with the uplifted hammer pause.

In this brief pause Robin gathered all his strength, tore himself free from the two men who were holding him, rushed towards the block, grabbed the hammer and brought it down with a crash on the hand holding the chisel, then hurled the hammer at the judge. Shouting at Tricket to follow him, he dived for the door and was away like lightning into the forest. The foresters went to follow him, but Mark and Marian were too clever for them. As soon as Robin disappeared they made as if to go after him, pushing six or seven of the onlookers in front of them, thus blocking the doorway. The foresters struggled and shouted, trying to get through the crowd, but by the time they got outside the barn Robin and Tricket were gone.

So Tricket still had all her paws and would live to be Robin's faithful friend for many years to come. But now they were both outside the law instead of sheltering in its arms. They were outlaws.

CHAPTER TWO

Into the Forest of Sherwood

A S Robin ran, his only thought was to get to Lastingham, two miles south-west of Hartoft, and hide in the crypt beneath the Abbey church which had lain unfinished for over a hundred years. There he would lie low till nightfall, till the hue and cry had died down.

He knew that the foresters would have their hounds on Tricket's scent, so he crossed-and-recrossed the stream before turning west. But at last he saw the Abbey, surrounded by the group of huts which made up the tiny village. Swiftly and silently he entered the church, lifted the trap door in the middle of the aisle and clambered down the rough ladder into the crypt, with Tricket close behind him; then quietly lowered the trap and felt his way carefully to the earthen floor below.

Inside the crypt all was dark except for the light from two tiny windows in each of the aisles, where the vast columns that supported the church above looked strong enough to carry a mountain on their shoulders.

Now at last he could breathe. Here for the time being he felt safe. But as he sat down to rest on a block of stone left by former workmen, he had a strange feeling that he was not alone. Someone was hiding behind one of the columns close to the altar. 'Come out,' he whispered. 'You need have no fear of me.'

At these words, an odd figure crept stealthily out from the shadows. He was little more than five feet tall, one shoulder was higher than the other and he walked with a limp. 'Do not be afraid,' said Robin quietly. 'I also am on the run. Who are you and where do you come from?'

'My name is Much,' said the little fellow. 'Called so because I had a fall when I was young, twisted my back and grew no bigger. I come from Mickleby, close to the sea. My father worked the village mill. But we cut millstones of our own and made a quern by which we earned ourselves an extra groat or two, grinding corn and beans for neighbours.'

'Against the law!' said Robin.

'I know it to my cost,' said Much. 'The farmer's servants came and took away our quern. We fought and lost. They beat my father senseless. I hurled a millstone at them, striking one fellow in the chest and felling him, breaking a rib or two. Then ran. And when I turned, I saw our home aflame. They had fired the thatch. I saw them drag my father out, and my mother kneeling beside him. I made for Lealholm, then turned left for Egton and so through Wheeldale by the ancient road. And here I am, waiting till dark. I am an outlaw.'

'It seems we are in the same sad pickle,' said Robin, and he told Much his own story. 'Let us sink or swim together. At nightfall I must return to fetch my bow and sword and some food. And say goodbye to two young people who are very dear to me.'

Late that night Robin made his way back to Hartoft, leaving Tricket with Much. It was dark outside, but there was still enough moon for him to move easily through the trees and into the yard.

As he lifted the latch of the farmhouse door, the watchdogs growled. But when he whispered to them, they recognised his voice and licked the hand he put down to them and made no more sound.

Softly he climbed the stairway, drew the curtain of Mark's room and knelt beside his bed, gently shaking him by the arm. Mark stirred and sat up, still half asleep.

''Tis me. 'Tis Robin, come to say goodbye and fetch my bow and sword. I have found a comrade in the crypt at Lastingham. A miller's son named Much. He also is on the run. Tomorrow we shall be gone.'

Now wide awake, Mark scrambled out of bed and together they crept into Marian's room, waking her just as Robin had awakened Mark. There they sat, hugging each other and whispering in the dark.

'Where will you go?' asked Mark.

'Westwards,' said Robin, ''till we meet the ancient road that runs along the country's spine. There are forests in the south, where bands of outlaws live and the soldiers cannot find them.'

'But how will you live?' said Marian.

'I shall have my bow,' said Robin. 'Much has his hunting knife and tinder box. The forests teem with food – the stag, the boar, the hare, the fish, the fowl. And running water. Bread we must beg or steal and now and then a mug of ale. More than enough.'

Then they were all three silent, thinking how lonely they were going to be.

'One day we shall meet again,' said Robin at last. 'I know not where or when, but I am sure.'

'One day,' said Marian, 'we shall come to you. We shall plan

in secret and slip away by night. You must tell us how you fare and where you hide.' Then she kissed Robin and said something that brought the tears flooding into his eyes. 'When I am older I shall marry you.'

They swore to tell no soul that Robin had returned to say goodbye and not to breathe a word that he might send messages from time to time, by secret means.

At last they stole downstairs into the pantry and Marian took a clean napkin and wrapped food in it; a loaf of new-baked bread and half a woodcock pie and honeycake and apples, then tied the cloth firmly at the top. And Mark took a bundle of rushlights and three tallow candles from the cupboard by the fireplace.

Then they crept out to Robin's hut, once more whispering to the watchdogs as they passed. Now Robin took his beloved bow and a quiver-full of arrows and buckled on his broadsword ready to depart. Then came the hardest thing of all, the last goodbye.

Mark and Marian were close to tears, but Robin took them in his arms and comforted them. 'Tomorrow morning, early, Much and I will make for Kirkdale. There we shall lie in the cave for one more night before striking out for Aldborough and the south. We mean to get as far away as possible by nightfall. One day, who knows, I may return. This life is full of change and chance.' Then he was gone and Mark and Marian were left shivering in the cold farmyard, knowing how sad they were going to be without him.

*   *   *   *

Robin was back at Lastingham long before dawn, with the candles and the rushlights and the clothfull of food. There in the crypt Much took his tinder box and lit a tiny gleam of light. Then they divided the pie and honeycake into equal parts and ate a small piece each, then gave a piece to Tricket. If she was coming with them they must share and share alike.

By sunrise, they were away, south-west to Kirkdale, to the cave that Robin knew so well, lying hidden all next day amongst the piles of bones – mammoth and bison and cave lion and sabre-toothed tiger and hyaenas and other creatures that had died thousands of years before – only creeping out at nightfall to move on west.

When morning came they reached the ruins of the camp at Aldborough with the sun behind them, then turned left along the road the Romans had built a thousand years before.

Sometimes they trapped a hare, sometimes took trout or grayling, sometimes Robin brought down a stag or a wild pig, which they skinned and gutted and cut up and gave to villagers

along the way in exchange for bowls of broth or bread and cheese or a warm night's sleep beside a cottage fire.

In those days, poor people could not afford meat. Mostly their food was bean soup and rough bread and home-brewed ale. All the deer and the wild pigs, the hares and the game birds belonged to the king or his lords, and if you were caught stealing them, you would be cruelly punished, like the foresters had tried to punish Tricket. So poor people were glad to get an occasional present of fish or meat from outlaws and give them a night's shelter in return, as long as they were out and away before morning.

So Robin and Much moved southwards, always on guard, skirting the great road, but never actually on it, always keeping to the greenwood by its side. From the shelter of the trees they saw travellers passing, at first very few, then, as they got further south, more and more – rich lords with their families and servants, soldiers moving from castle to castle, great churchmen on their way to visit some abbey, Fountains near Ripon, or St Mary's in York, or Selby further south; or merchants selling salt or soap or woollen cloth. And always they lay hidden until the road was clear again.

Through Tadcaster and Castleton they passed, and there, for the first time, they learned of the continual warfare between the Sheriff of Nottingham and the outlaws of Sherwood Forest; of how he had captured and hanged many of them, and had sworn to clear them from the forest. And of how some of the outlaws, frightened of being tortured, had gone over to the Sheriff's side and were now helping him and his men to hunt down their old comrades.

At last they found themselves in the forest itself, and it was here that they had their first adventure. They were moving through thick undergrowth when Tricket suddenly flattened her ears and gave a low growl. They stopped and listened. At first they could hear nothing, but then faint and far off came the familiar swish of bow-strings being loosed and every now and then a ragged cheer. Now they went forward twice as carefully as before, doing their best to make no sound.

Soon the shooting and cheering were very near, and suddenly they were at the edge of a great open ride, more like meadow-land than forest, two hundred yards or more in length and nearly half as wide. At the end nearest to them, standing or kneeling or squatting on their heels, were eighteen or twenty men in torn and ragged clothes, all with bows and quivers full of arrows, their broadswords lying on the turf around them.

At the other end, a hundred yards or so away, supported by a pole set in the ground, was a target like an old worn mattress, painted with coloured rings. And fastened to its centre, creamy white, a wand of peeled willow, with three or four men

17

standing beside it to mark the scores and bring the arrows back to the bowmen. They were 'Splitting-the-Wand', the most difficult of all archery contests. The wand was less than an inch across, no thicker than a broom-handle, so the man who could split it with a single arrow must indeed be a fine archer. And none had yet succeeded, for the wand stood still intact.

At last Robin and Much stepped out from the trees into the open. Swiftly the outlaws strung their bows and seized their swords. But Robin was not afraid. 'Good friends,' he said. 'It seems we are brothers in the self-same trade. My name is Robin Hood. And this is Much, a miller's son. We come from further

north, both outlawed.' Then he asked if he could chance his arm and try to split the wand.

The leader of the outlaws, a sturdy fellow named Will Scarlet, turned to his men to know their wishes. 'No!' said one or two. 'We want no strangers here.' But most said, 'Let the northern fellow try.' So Robin unslung his sword, drew an arrow from its quiver and stepped to the mark. For a few seconds he stroked the bow as if asking it to guide the arrow home, then laid the arrow on the string, took careful aim and loosed. With lightning speed the arrow flew, the point struck home, the willow wand was split, the two halves falling sideways, left and right.

The outlaws gasped. They could hardly believe what they had seen. They were supposed to be the finest archers in Sherwood, yet here was this young stranger beating them at their chosen game.

'Well shot!' Will Scarlet cried. 'Well shot indeed!'

'But could you do it twice?' said one of the men who had not wanted to let Robin join in the shooting.

'I might well do it thrice,' said Robin laughing. 'Set up another wand and let me try.'

So the outlaws took another wand and peeled it and set it up in the middle of the target. Once more Robin shot. Once more the arrow pierced the wand, but this time did not cleave it.

There it stuck, fast in the willow. Then he took a third arrow, hoping to make good his boast. He had never before split the wand three times, perhaps he had been foolish to say he might. Now there was no escape; the outlaws held their breath, the bow was bent, the arrow sat upon the string, then flew, splitting the wand an inch below the one he shot before. The two halves fell apart, leaving the arrows fastened to the target.

The outlaws cheered. They could not help themselves. At first they had wanted Robin to fail, for they did not care for rivals, especially from another part of the country. But this shooting was no accident, this man was the greatest bowman they had ever seen and they clustered round him, praising him and examining his bow, running their hands over it and smoothing the string.

So Robin and Much and Tricket joined the outlaws of Sherwood and Will Scarlet begged Robin to become their leader, 'For,' said he, 'until you came, I was the best by far. But now I know that I have met my master.' And he and the others shook Robin by the hand, each asking him if he would take command.

Before Robin would agree, he said they must get to know more about each other. He wanted to know their names and where they came from and why they had been outlawed. He also wanted to be sure they would wish to obey the kind of rules that he had been taught to live by, and not be just a band of clumsy robbers. To this the outlaws agreed. But first, they said, they must take Robin and Much to their forest hideout and give them food and drink. So they gathered their swords and bows and quivers and away they went.

Their shelter lay against a high stone cliff. It was roofed over with a sort of mat made of birch poles lashed together and thatched, then hauled up and fastened to tree trunks on either side; with a curtain of deer-skin laced across its front. Outside there smouldered a fire with a huge iron pot hanging over it and, near the fire, a vast oak table, and under the table wooden buckets filled with water from a nearby spring.

On a smaller table stood a pestle and mortar, and a stirring stick, and baking pans and meat hooks, and a griddle, and a set of wooden bowls, and a pile of platters and a dressing board. In fact, everything you could possibly need for preparing food and cooking it, all mixed up together, but everything in reach.

The outlaws welcomed Robin and Much to their home and drank their health. They supped on baked trout and venison lapped in batter and fresh hazel-nut bread, washed down with home-brewed ale. And they gave Tricket a nice big bone, the first she had tasted since the foresters captured her.

When supper was over and Robin came to ask each man why he had been outlawed, they stepped up one by one as Will

Scarlet called their names; Jack Noakes, Ben Frow, Adam Carpenter, Gilbert Payn, John Silke, Will Curstan, Simon Scales and so on. And here are some of the answers that they gave to Robin's questions:

'For bringing down a stag and getting caught carrying it home. We fought the foresters and wounded one of them. One of our lot was killed.'

'For hunting boar. My wife and children cried for food.'

'We kept a pig on our small patch and gathered acorns for it. The verderers came upon us and we ran. They killed my dog.'

'My father was a poacher all his life. When I was old enough I joined him. Last year he died, here in the forest. He is buried yonder. I carry on the trade. 'Tis in my blood.'

'I stole wild honey and fermented it for mead. I took the beeswax for my bow and bowstring.'

'My cottage roof fell in. I cut a birch tree down to mend it.'

So the answers came. No-one made excuses, no-one tried to lay the blame on anyone else.

Some of the men were maimed. Gilbert Bolle showed his right hand with three fingers missing, cut off by the foresters so that he should never again pull a bowstring. The same had happened to Thomas Warin, but a blacksmith friend had made him a glove with a steel claw worked by a spring: with this he could pull almost as well as with real fingers. Harvey Buleman had lost an ear, John Silke an eye.

When Robin had heard their stories, he and Much told theirs. Then, as the fire burned low, Robin gathered the men around him and gave them his ideas of how they would have to change their way of life if he was to become their leader.

'We must have rules to live by and we must keep them. We must know who we fight and why. We must be an army not a ragged mob. And we must cling together man to man. We must never rob the poor and needy. Only the rich; then only those who have too much and who got their wealth unfairly. Many rich folk are generous and noble. We must never harm the aged or women or children, and we must be ever mindful that we live under the hand of God. It is the law that sins, not us. We only seek to change it. This is the greenwood oath and all must swear it.'

He spoke very simply, using no big words or fine phrases, and as they listened the men warmed to him. This was the kind of leader they had been waiting for, and they warmed to him even more as he continued:

'We need not kill the travellers we rob. I have a better plan. Capture the rich and bring them home to dine. And make them welcome. Then find what gold they carry and make them pay for what they have received. If in their saddle bags we find two hundred pounds, take half and send them on their way, saying: "It is more blessed to give than to receive. The price we charge for food and drink is high, but what better table have you ever found? What better tale to tell your children?"'

Then he asked them a question which they found hard to answer. 'When do you go to church? And where? When do you eat the body of Christ and drink his blood and hear his promise spoken once again? Though we are put outside the law of man, we dare not be outlaws from Heaven.'

Will Scarlet and his men had no answer to this. They had been too busy to think of such things. Sometimes they would murmur a prayer before going to sleep or speak a few words about Jesus and his mother when they had to bury a dead comrade. But it was a long time since they had taken the feast of bread and wine which we call Communion. And even if they had wanted to take it they had no priest to give it to them.

'We must catch a tame priest and hold him captive,' said Robin.

The idea of catching a tame priest was so funny that the outlaws laughed, but in a warm and happy way. For it was comforting to think that even if they were outside the laws of man they might still be welcome in the arms of the Church and be shielded by the mercy of the great God who ruled both Heaven and Earth; that when they died they might still be citizens of Paradise.

And Will Scarlet, who until then had been their captain, gave up his claim, handing to Robin the silver horn which was the mark and badge of leadership. For whenever their leader was in danger, he had only to blow three blasts upon his horn and all the outlaws would come rushing to his aid. Then Robin embraced Will and every man in the company took the greenwood oath and swore to be loyal to Robin, even unto death.

So the army grew. At first barely twenty, but then, as they heard what was happening, others joined, until they numbered more than a hundred.

BUT now I must stop a moment to tell you who Robin was, where and when he was born, something about the world he was born into, and who the two children were who helped to save Tricket from having her paw chopped off. So here goes!

Nobody knows exactly when Robin was born, but we think it was about 1170 during the reign of King Henry II, somewhere on the North Yorkshire Moors. In those days there was no settled border between England and Scotland, so the north was a specially dangerous place. Every so often the Scots would come rushing down through Northumberland and Durham into Yorkshire, killing people and burning their houses, and the English would have to gather an army together and drive them back.

Robin's father had been killed in one of these raids and his mother had died soon afterwards. So Robin was adopted by a kindly farmer who lived at a tiny place called Hartoft, tucked away on the western edge of Cropton Forest, about seven miles north of Pickering and a little to the west.

Hartoft is a very old place alongside a clear stream. People have lived and worked there for thousands of years: hunting and fishing, fashioning tools of bone and stone and bronze and iron, learning how to make fire, to warm themselves in winter, to drive away wild animals and later on for cooking; burying their dead on the mountain-sides above and setting up great stones for worshipping-places, which you can still see.

There was no room in the farmhouse to take Robin in properly, so they put him into a tiny outhouse. But he had his meals with the family and became part of it, making himself handy around the farmyard and in the garden. All this he greatly enjoyed. But what he liked most was practising with his bow and arrows. This he had learned from his father, who had made him a tiny bow of hazelwood when he was seven years old. His father taught him how to string it and how to place the arrow on the string; how to aim and how to push the bow away from the string, not try to pull the string away from the bow. 'One day your bow may save your life,' his father had said. 'A man must know how to defend his home and his family and his village, especially with the bow. Of all weapons the bow is best because it can strike the enemy at a distance, and prevent him coming nearer.'

Robin put in a lot of practice with his bow, sometimes four or five hours a day, so that by the time he was fourteen years old he could shoot an arrow nearly two hundred yards and could aim so well that he could hit the middle of the target four or five times out of ten. As he grew older he got better still, until his name became famous in all the north of England.

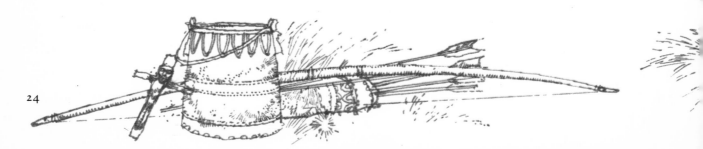

Now, as I told you, the farmer had these two children, Mark and Marian, and they loved being with Robin, especially when he was practising with his bow. They would stand near to the tree he was shooting at, and when he had shot ten or twelve arrows they would pull them out and take them back to him so that he could start shooting all over again. And they would tell him how close he had got to the circle of white cloth they had fastened to the tree. In the end they got Robin to make each of them a bow and teach them to use it, also how to use a broadsword and quarterstaff – that was a strong pole made of oak or ash which was often used instead of a sword, especially at village fairs when the men wanted to show off their strength.

So, although they were still so young, Mark and Marian became very good at archery and sword fighting. In fact they were soon shooting arrows more than a hundred yards and getting them very close to the circle. Marian was even better than Mark. She was a real tomboy, tall and strong, yet quick as lightning, especially with her sword. Indeed, she would often challenge Robin himself and he would find it quite difficult to hold her off. Some brothers would have been jealous of such a sister, but Mark was proud of her and whenever she beat him to his knees and put her sword to his throat pretending to kill him he would jump up and hug her, enjoying the fun of it.

Of course the foresters were jealous of Robin because he knew more about the forest than they did. His father had taught him the names of all the birds and wild animals and how to recognise the different sounds they made both in the day time and at night, and how to imitate them. And he had learned to patch his clothes with old pieces of green and brown cloth so that he merged in with everything around him. And he had hiding places in tree-tops and under overhanging rocks where he would lie for hours watching and listening as secretly and silently as a wild animal.

And they were more jealous still because he was a better archer than they were. So jealous in fact, that they started looking for some way to get him and his dog Tricket into trouble, and at last they succeeded, by turning them both into outlaws. But now I must tell you how Little John came to join Robin's band and how he became second-in-command.

CHAPTER THREE

Robin meets Little John and Friar Tuck

ROBIN knew many of the forests in the far north, especially those near his home at Hartoft, but Sherwood was new to him and it took him some time to learn its glades and rides and tracks and how the rivers flowed through it on their journey to the sea.

One day he came to a stream with a narrow bridge across it, just a few poles lashed together, almost too narrow for one man to cross, let alone two. Just as he was stepping on to it, a huge black-bearded fellow with shoulders like an ox came out of the trees on the other side, carrying an oak staff six feet long.

'I'll trouble you to step aside 'till I have crossed,' he shouted to Robin as he came up to the bridge.

'I turn aside for no man,' answered Robin. 'Hereabouts men turn aside for me.'

'Then let us try the matter with our staves,' said the bearded fellow. 'Let him who throws the other in the stream have right of way.'

'Gladly,' replied Robin. 'But give me time to cut a staff.' And he drew his sword and hacked a branch from an ash tree that grew nearby and trimmed it of leaves and twigs. Then threw down his bow and sword and quiver.

Stepping on to the bridge together, one at either end, they advanced to meet each other. Robin, being light and quick, made the first stroke, aiming it high to crack the bearded fellow's head. Black-beard warded off the blow and in his turn gave Robin a great thwack on his left arm, nearly breaking it. 'Hello,' thought Robin, as they locked staves and tried to overset each other into the stream, 'I've got my hands full here.'

Then he gave Black-beard a rap across his ear that made it sing, and followed it with another on his staff, nearly knocking it out of his hand. Indeed, Robin used every trick he knew, but Black-beard laughed and parried every stroke. So they moved

backwards and forwards, first one gaining the advantage then the other, until at last, advancing to the middle of the bridge, Black-beard gave Robin an upward blow that lifted him into the air, right off the bridge and splash, head over heels into the water!

As Robin looked up, streaming wet, the bearded fellow was laughing and offering his staff to haul him back on to dry land. There Robin embraced him. 'You beat me fair and square,' he said. 'I dub you King of the Quarterstaff. What is your name and where do you come from?'

'John Little is my name,' said the bearded giant. 'I come from west of here, from Hathersage. I was caught poaching in the farmer's fishpond. Five or six set on me and beat me black and blue. But I gave better than I got. I broke a head or two, and learning that you welcome outlaws hereabouts, I started walking east and here I am.' Then he laid his huge hand on Robin's shoulder. 'You have a mighty heart inside that slender

body.' And they clasped hands and swore to be friends, and John Little became Robin's right-hand man.

'But we must change your name,' said Robin. 'John Little falls awkwardly from the tongue and no way suits your bulk. I shall re-christen you. Henceforth be Little John.'

So Little John joined the band and the outlaws welcomed him as gladly as they had welcomed Robin. He was so brave and strong and, next to Robin, the finest bowman. He was six feet seven inches tall and his bow four inches longer, the longest longbow ever made. He could shoot fourteen or fifteen arrows in a minute, the fastest archer in the land save Robin. Not shooting wildly but all aimed and all clapped squarely in the clout, which is the bowman's target.

The longbow was a terrible weapon. Well-aimed arrows flew fast and true, and their hardened points had such hitting power that they could pierce a knight's armour a hundred yards away. At famous battles like Crécy and Poitiers and Agincourt, a small force of two hundred and fifty archers could shoot eighty thousand arrows within half an hour. These fighting archers wore no armour, only a strong leather cap. And they had no horses to bother with, so they could move lightly and swiftly; and often one of their arrows would go right through a knight and his horse and be sticking out on the other side.

For two hundred years, until the coming of gunpowder, the longbow was the master of the battlefield. And the English were the masters of the longbow. Children were taught to use it from an early age and laws were passed which said that every man and boy must practise shooting every week.

*   *   *   *

A few weeks after Little John joined the outlaws Robin found the very man he was looking for to be their priest. His name was Michael Tuck, a monk from Fountains Abbey near to Ripon. And now, in case you don't know the meaning of the words 'monk' and 'abbey', I must tell you something about the Church in Robin's time and how the Christian story had got twisted out of shape and how men often used it in the wrong way.

You see the story taught that God had sent Jesus down to earth to help people out of their troubles and to heal them when they were sick and encourage them to live better lives. He and his disciples were a tiny team and he was their captain. And when he was crucified his eleven disciples tried to carry on his work. But they feared that when their own turn came to die his teachings would be forgotten and it would be as if he had never lived.

For a long time they tried to go on living holy lives all by themselves, in huts and caves and even on top of marble columns. Then they thought that if they formed themselves into fresh teams and built places called abbeys where each team could be together, their singing and praying would be stronger than if they lived separately. Besides, they would no longer be lonely. And this idea spread all over Europe and hundreds of these abbeys came to be built. And the men who lived in them were called monks and when they joined they had to promise to obey the abbey rules and live like Jesus had done, praying and teaching and healing the sick.

Each abbey had a big church for singing and praying in, and a dining room for eating and a dormitory for sleeping: also a kitchen and a pantry and an infirmary and a guest house and

workshops and storerooms and so on; everything they could possibly need.

Some of the monks spent their whole lives worshipping God at special times all through the day and night while their helpers worked in the gardens and orchards or out on the hills looking after the sheep. Sometimes there were over a hundred praying monks and five hundred working ones in a single abbey. And every abbey had a high wall round it. It was like a complete village without any women or children living in it. Only men.

The one in charge of the abbey, the sort of headmaster, was called the abbot. He had a lodging all to himself. And there were special rules for how the monks should live, when they should pray and when they should eat and sleep and when they should work in the fields and so on. And they all dressed alike in rough woollen gowns and woollen stockings, with a rope or leather girdle round their waist. And a circle of hair in the middle of their heads was shaved off as a sort of trade mark.

Now as time went on, many of these abbeys forgot all about Jesus and his teachings. They only wanted to get richer and have more power over people's lives. And one of the richest and most powerful in the whole of England was this one called Fountains, in Yorkshire. And it was from Fountains that Michael Tuck had run away and was now living by himself in a little cave in the middle of Sherwood Forest.

Michael was the son of a butcher in the village of Pateley Bridge and when he was seventeen years old he joined the Abbey as a novice, which is someone who goes in to be trained. And in time he became a full-fledged monk and he was a hard worker and a good strong singer and a deep believer and a credit to the Abbey.

But one day he asked why abbeys needed to become so rich and powerful and why they needed to steal whole villages from the poor and break up their families and turn them out to starve. 'Is that what Jesus meant when he said, "Another commandment give I unto you. Love one another"?' he asked.

When he heard what Michael had been saying the Abbot got very angry and had him brought up in front of the court which met every morning in a part of the Abbey called the Chapter House.

But Michael wouldn't give in. He said he thought that many abbeys had strayed a long way from the truth and that Fountains was just as bad as some of the others. In fact he said he thought it had become very greedy and had forgotten all the wonderful things that Jesus had taught. And he said he thought it ought to pull its socks up before it was too late. At this the Abbot went very red in the face and tried to hit Michael with his crozier. But Michael ducked and that made the Abbot lose his balance and fall over. And when they had picked him up and dusted him down and put him back on his throne, he said that as a punishment for saying such wicked things Michael must be shut away in the Abbey prison for three months with nothing but bread and water to eat and drink. And six monks tried to lay hold of him and take him to the prison and lock him in.

But Michael was very strong and he fought them off and knocked them flying and ran from the Chapter House and escaped into the country, travelling South and finally settling all by himself in a little cave beside a stream in Sherwood Forest, resisting anyone who tried to shift him. He did not hate the Abbot or the monks. Indeed, he felt sorry for them because he knew they had their minds fixed on the wrong things, that they were wanting to get rich instead of staying poor as Jesus had said they must if they wanted to serve God properly. But now let us get back to our story.

One day Robin came to a river he would have to cross if he was to be back in camp by supper time. But after the September rains it was swollen so high and rushing along so fast that at first he thought the only possible way to cross would be to jump in and swim.

Then he noticed a strange figure sitting on the bank dressed in a rough brown habit with sandals on his feet. By his side lay his bow and quiver and his broadsword, and he was fishing with a net on the end of a long pole. It was Michael fishing for his supper.

When he saw how broad and strong he looked, Robin said to himself, 'Here's a man strong enough to carry me across – with luck I shouldn't even get my feet wet!' So he walked up to Michael and tapped him on the shoulder.

'Fellow,' he said. 'You fish in outlaw waters. The fish you catch belong by rights to us. But if you carry me to the other side we will give you permission to fish our rivers once a month.'

'I take only what I need for food,' replied Michael bluntly. 'The fish and fowl are free. But I will carry you across. Climb on my back and mind you hold your bow and quiver high.' Then he took off his sandals and stockings and tucked his skirts up into his belt, and Robin climbed onto him pick-a-back fashion. And Michael waded into the water, buffeting it aside with lusty sinews, finally setting Robin down on the opposite bank as dry as a bone.

Now Michael did not like the way Robin had spoken to him. He had as much right to fish the stream as anyone else and he certainly was not going to ask permission from a bunch of outlaws. So he thought he would pay Robin out and this is how he did it.

'You look a strong young fellow,' he said. 'Do you think you could carry me across as easily as I carried you? If you can, I will

bring you back and set you down on this side once again. There now! I challenge you!'

Robin had never yet refused to accept a challenge, so he laid aside his bow and quiver and came to the water's edge. Then took Michael on his back and stepped into the water.

He could tell by looking at him that Michael was pretty heavy, but as they moved towards the middle of the stream he seemed to grow heavier still so that, with the water rushing past, it was as much as he could do to keep his feet, and the sweat poured down his forehead and he was soon puffing and blowing like a grampus. But at last he staggered up the opposite bank and set Michael down.

'There,' he said. 'You thought I'd never do it. Now comes your turn. Carry me back and set me on my way!'

Once more Michael waded into the stream, carrying Robin as easily as if he were a two-year-old. But suddenly, giving a great jerk of his spine and shaking Robin's arms from round his neck, he hurled him three or four feet into the air and splash, head over ears into the river!

Robin fell face downwards and disappeared from view and it was some seconds before he managed to get his head above water again. When he did so he saw Michael standing up to his waist in the stream shaking with laughter.

'You say I must beg leave to come a-fishing in your brook,' said Michael. 'Must I now beg leave to fish you out?' And he put his great foot on Robin's chest, holding him firmly in the water.

'No,' shouted Robin in return. 'You can come fishing when you will. I give you best.' So Michael bent down and hauled him up on to the bank. Then, still laughing, helped him squeeze the water out of his clothes.

'I fancy you had better get before a fire before you take a

chill,' he said. 'Be on your way and God go with you.'

'You must come too,' said Robin. 'Our camp is but a mile or two from here. My outlaws are good men and true. We need a priest.' Then, as he waited for Michael to answer, 'What must we call you?'

'My name is Michael. Michael Tuck. Lately of Fountains Abbey. I quarrelled with the Abbot and we parted company. Since then I have lived alone, here in the greenwood.'

'Come join with me and my brave company,' said Robin, holding out his hand. 'We miss the word of God. We miss the bread and wine.' And he took Michael's huge hand and shook it and they swore to be friends. That was one of the nicest things about Robin. He never minded being beaten. At one time or another he fought with a butcher, a potter, a tanner, a tinker, a shepherd, and a Yorkshire pindar and was beaten by them all. But he soon shook hands and praised the men who had beaten him. That is why his men loved him and that is why he gathered together such a strong and loyal band and that is why he was such a great leader.

So Michael joined the outlaws. They made him a tiny chapel in the greenwood, with an altar and a cross. And the morning after he came, he said Mass and the outlaws all knelt down and he went from man to man with the wine cup, and Clement Glose made up a platter of bread cut into tiny pieces and every man took bread and wine in memory of the little supper that the greatest of all outlaws had shared with his twelve comrades long long ago, in an upper room in old Jerusalem.

And Tricket sat at the end of the line looking up with her great brown eyes, so she had a morsel of bread and a sip of wine along with the others, because Jesus loved animals as well as men and women. Indeed, if he and his mother had not escaped to Egypt on a donkey, King Herod might have killed him when he was a tiny baby.

At the end of his life he rode into Jerusalem on another donkey as if to say thank you to all donkeys. Some people say that the second donkey was the son of the one his mother had used to carry him safely into Egypt all those years ago. And others say that he meant to put an extra verse into the Beatitudes, 'Blessed are the animals for they are as important as man, and deserve to be loved and cared for.' But he forgot.

In later days monks who left their monasteries and went about the countryside doing good and helping people like Jesus had done were called 'Friars', which means 'Brothers'. But that is exactly what Michael had been doing for twenty years and more, here in the greenwood. So he was the first to think of it. That is why he is always known as 'Friar Tuck' instead of 'Brother Michael'. And that is what we shall call him for the rest of our story – Friar Tuck.

CHAPTER FOUR

The Winter Cave

IT was Will Sawyer who first thought of finding a different place to shelter. For it was a cruel life in winter when the trees and bushes were mostly bare and it was hard to stay hidden, and it was bitterly cold even inside their hide. So many of their band had been caught and hanged, so many maimed and blinded. Some had even lost their way in snow-storms and were found weeks later, frozen to death.

Will had been a woodman, skilled at felling trees and cutting them into planks and splitting them with wedges and trimming them with his adze. He had been caught shooting a stag and skinning it in the hut where he kept his tools, and when he was brought before the Court the judge had ordered that his right hand should be cut off so that he could never go poaching again. So he left home and joined the outlaws. But he knew every inch of the forest and when Robin talked of going underground, his eyes lit up.

'There is a cave,' he said, 'deep in the forest, north of here. My father took me there when I was young, but made me swear to keep it secret. It is at the end of a downward-sloping track and the entrance is a rock that turns when you lean against it, as if it were hung on hinges. When you go within, you close it by pushing on the other side. A stream of clear water bubbles through it, and between cracks in the rocks above, a little light shines through, enough to see a maze of smaller caves leading out of the main one, with many clefts and galleries. And it is clean inside because no animal could ever find the way to enter. If I could find that place again we could winter there in warmth and safety.'

They searched for weeks and were on the point of giving up when Harvey Buleman found it. First the long downward slope and the face of rock with long creeper hanging over it. Pushing against the face in several places, first gently then firmly, a shower of sand suddenly began to trickle from above and the rock began to move. Slowly at first, then gathering speed, it

swung round on its pivot. And there inside was the cave, just as Will had seen it years before.

Harvey whistled to the others and they all came running, with Will Sawyer in the lead. And when they saw it they went wild with excitement.

'This is the place,' said Will as they entered. 'Enough to house a hundred outlaws safe and sound all through the longest winter.'

So it was here that they made their second home, cleaning it and fitting it out with everything they needed: a long sleeping place with rough canvas mattresses; a kitchen with a vast fireplace and a supply of clean water from the spring; carpenter's and blacksmith's shops and a store-room for wine and salt and beans and oatmeal and dried fish; a workshop where Tom Fletcher made bows and arrows and finished them off with wild goose feathers and heads of Sheffield steel; a sick bay with honey and herbs and ointments and splints and bandages and the set of sharp knives they sometimes had to use to get an arrow-head out of an arm or leg or shoulder, and needles and thread for stitching the edges of a wound together

after they had made the patient drunk; and a stable to hold half a dozen horses. And most important of all a washing place, a long stone channel sloping downwards, with the stream always running through it and, at the far end, some simple latrines cut from oak beams; and everything falling with the water into a pool far below in the centre of the hill.

Lastly, another tiny chapel with altar and cross and a rough cushion to kneel on as the outlaws came up one by one to take communion, and a tiny cupboard scooped in the wall to hold the bread and wine.

Here they lived from October till March, only going out to snare woodcock or snipe or swans or cranes or river mallard, or to take wagons to the coast and bring back loads of fish already salted down.

Sometimes peasants walking along the forest ways would hear a faint knocking from inside the hill or the soft ring of a hammer on an anvil, or quiet singing. And sometimes they would see a faint wisp of smoke rising from amongst the trees, but they kept their mouths shut or pretended they had seen or heard it in their sleep.

CHAPTER FIVE

Sir Richard of the Lea

ONE stormy autumn evening, Little John and Much and Will Scarlet were hiding amongst the trees that lined the Great North Road, waiting to see if they could capture some wealthy traveller and bring him back to their forest to dine. For two hours they had waited and seen nothing but country-folk; ploughmen, swineherds, quarrymen, shepherds, carpenters, stonemasons and such like, all wending their way home after a hard day's work in forest, field or workshop.

From the north, a fine rain was driving through the trees and it was growing dark. Already they were half-soaked and soon would be half-frozen. 'Duty is duty,' whispered Little John. 'But enough is enough. I vote for the fireside and a good square meal.'

'Wise man,' said Much. 'I add my voice to yours.'

'And I add mine,' said Will.

They rose and stretched their arms and stamped their feet to warm their blood and loosen up their joints. Suddenly they paused and listened. Between the gusts of wind and the creaking of the branches overhead, came the sound of a horse's hooves and the faint jingling of harness. Once more they knelt and peered between the bushes.

Through the mist they saw a horseman beating his way into the teeth of the wind. The horse's ribs showed through its ragged coat and it looked ready to drop from exhaustion. The rider was a knight, wrapped in a tattered cloak, his chain-mail glinting in the rain.

'What think you?' whispered Much.

'We can but try,' said Little John as he stepped out into the road.

Seeing Little John, the horse stumbled and nearly fell, but John grabbed the bridle and steadied it, while the rider, caught by surprise, drew his sword half out of its scabbard.

'Put up your bright sword, for the rain will rust it,' said Little

John, leading the horse off the road into the trees. When Much saw the knight and the poor, raw-boned horse he pulled a wry face.

'Scarcely worth robbing,' he murmured.

'Things are not always what they seem,' said Little John. Then, to the knight, 'Sir, you have travelled far. You and your horse are cold and wet and hungry. We offer food and shelter and a royal welcome. Come, follow us.'

The knight slid from his saddle and stood there dripping wet.

'Both horse and rider will be fed,' said Much. 'Our leader is no skinflint.' And he took the horse by the bridle and led the way into the forest, followed by the knight and Will Scarlet, with Little John bringing up the rear. Thus they moved on with no-one speaking, until they drew near to the cave.

'Your host will want to know your name,' said Little John. 'What shall we call you?'

'I am Sir Richard of the Lea, unfortunate and unhappy,' said the knight. Then, after a pause, 'What is your leader called?'

'He is the Prince of Outlaws, Robin Hood,' said Will.

Before Sir Richard could recover from his astonishment, Little John walked forward and pushed against the rock face that now towered above them.

Noiselessly and as if by magic, half the hillside seemed to roll away and they exchanged the raw damp of the forest for the cosy firelight of the cave. Then at a touch from Will, the rock swung back into place, so perfectly was it balanced and so completely did it fill the entrance to the cave.

For a few moments the knight stood and stared as if he were dreaming. There in the middle of the cave a great fire smouldered, with a tripod set above it and a cauldron full of steaming broth. On one side stood a vast oak table laden with silver cups and flagons and other fine tableware. There were benches and rough stools and blocks of stone, set ready for a meal, with tallow candles and rush-lights in silver holders all a-glimmer. And five or six smaller caverns led away into the shadows and the whole scene was full of men, some winding bowstrings and oiling them with wax and tallow, some putting an edge on their daggers, some making new bracers; and all calm and orderly as if they had been living like this all their lives.

As Sir Richard and his escort came to a halt a few yards from the fire, Much led the weary horse into the stable to rub it down and give it a well-earned feed.

'Robin,' shouted Little John. 'We have a guest, Sir Richard of the Lea.'

Robin was sitting with an oaken board across his knees and a glue pot at his feet, cutting goose feathers to the proper shape and sticking them on to a pile of arrows that lay beside him.

Now he rose, holding out his hand as if to greet an old and valued friend.

'Welcome, Sir Richard, to our humble fireside. You look cold and hungry. Throw off your cloak. Come nearer to the fire.' Then, calling to the cook, 'Bring wine and let us drink to our guest. And then to supper.'

Suddenly, the whole place sprang to life, and the cook started dipping his ladle into the cauldron and serving broth as the outlaws lined up with their bowls and took great hunks of rye-bread from a wooden bin, breaking the loaves by hand. Then wine was being poured from silver flagons and supper was in full swing.

Robin sat at one side of the table with Sir Richard on his right hand and Little John on his left. But first every man stood and crossed himself as Friar Tuck said grace. 'Pro hoc cibo benedicite benedictum per Jesus Christum Dominum Nostrum Amen.'

The food was of the best, fit for a king – roast venison, piping hot and done to a turn; eels boiled in oil, then sliced and fried with comfrey leaves; plover baked in batter; and fine roast boar

well browned, with breadcrumbs. Then cheese and nuts and apples and plums and peaches, all washed down with Gascon wine well mulled, or home-brewed ale in tankards.

The outlaws did full justice to the food, and no wonder! One meal a day was Robin's rule. No over-eating! Every man must be in hard condition, ready to hunt or fight or run.

When supper was over, Robin thought it was time to tell Sir Richard that although they had made him so welcome, the meal he had just eaten must now be paid for. 'It is our custom here when entertaining guests to search their saddle-bags, to find what gold they carry. We then divide the spoils. One half to them, one half to us. That seems a fair division.'

'Then I fear you will come poorly off with me,' said Sir Richard. 'Ten shillings is all I own. That you are welcome to.'

''Tis true,' said Much, who had already been through the knight's saddle-bags, and he tossed a few silver coins on to the table.

'How comes a knight so poor?' said Robin. 'Have you no castle, lands or cattle?'

'A year ago I had,' said Sir Richard. 'But then ill luck befell

me. My only son got caught in a brawl and killed the man he fought with. My lad was not to blame. Nevertheless, he was thrown into prison. I had to find four hundred pounds to buy his freedom. I had no ready money. I tried to borrow, but my friends turned from me. My only hope lay in St Mary's Abbey.'

'Of York?' asked Robin.

'Yes,' said Sir Richard. 'Of York. I knew the Abbot there.'

'A man ungodly, greedy, fierce and proud,' said Robin.

'Yes,' said Sir Richard, 'but wealthy. The Abbey swims in gold. I went to him for help. He gave it me on terms too hard to meet.'

'What terms?' asked Friar Tuck.

'A loan, on pledge. I put my all in pawn – lands, castle, cattle, all I have. The term, a full year from the day we signed and sealed. My son was freed. But now the year is up, I cannot pay. I am on my way to York to beg a few months' grace. But fear I shall not win it.'

'You never will,' said Friar Tuck. 'I know that Abbot well. He came to Fountains once and cuffed the kitchener for spilling wine. 'Twas not the fellow's fault. The jug was over-full. He stumbled. I fear you go to York on a wild goose chase. They will have your lands, your all.'

For a few moments the outlaws were silent. Then Robin put into words what they were all thinking. 'Sir Richard,' he said. 'I, too, will make a bargain with you.' Then, turning to Will Scarlet, 'Go to the strong box, Will, and fetch four hundred pounds. And find a horse and armour and a suit of clothing fit for our good friend's station. We will send him on his way to keep his pledge with the Abbot. Now then, Sir Knight, what surety can you give?'

'None,' said Sir Richard, 'save my word and bond, given on the holy name of Mary, the mother of Jesus. 'Tis all I have to give. For a full year. And then I will repay you.'

'Agreed,' said Robin and the outlaws echoed him, 'Agreed, agreed.' And Tricket wagged her tail as if she too agreed.

'And now to sleep,' said Friar Tuck. 'The hour draws on apace. We must be up betimes to see our good friend fairly horsed and harnessed.'

'He will need a squire,' said Little John. 'Whoever heard of a knight without a squire!'

'Why not yourself?' said Robin. And suddenly the whole cave echoed to a roar of laughter. The thought of a squire six feet seven inches tall and weighing seventeen stone was so funny. But the idea appealed to Little John and he agreed. And so, still laughing, they retired to their sleeping places and soon all was quiet except for the bubbling of the spring as it ran through its channel and tumbled into the hollow below.

Early next morning Will Scarlet went into the wardrobe and

chose a costume for Sir Richard – a rose-coloured knee-length tunic with embroidered edge, a cloak of apple-green with golden brooch, a handsome jewelled sword-belt, woollen hose and dove-soft leather shoes. And to crown all, a sword of finest temper. But when the knight began to put them on, Little John said, 'Stay! I have a better notion. Let us travel humbly, poorly clad, to test this Abbot of his charity.'

So instead of dressing Sir Richard in the fine clothes they had chosen, they let him travel ragged and untidy just as he had arrived the night before. And Little John put on a suit to match, well-worn, in places even threadbare. The fine clothes they packed in a bundle which they strapped to the pommel of Little John's horse. And so they set out for York with many goodbyes and hand-clasps.

York was a hundred miles away along the Great North Road. Four days they travelled, sheltering at night in sheepfolds or in charcoal-burners' huts or beside the fires of friendly villagers, until at last they reached the city and the River Ouse. They passed up Skeldergate, then crossed the river, hugging its northern bank until they reached Marygate, which led to the Abbey. Taking down the bundle and tying their horses to an iron ring in the Abbey wall, they went to the postern gate and knocked.

When he saw them, the porter hesitated. He was used to poor people asking for food and shelter for the night, but not down-at-heel rascals like these asking to see the Abbot himself. The Abbot was all-powerful, like the king. Some people had been known to wait for days or even weeks before they were admitted to his presence.

But when Sir Richard gave his name and said he had come to pay his debt, and when he saw the determined look on Little John's face, the porter went at once to tell the Abbot.

The Abbot was at supper in the refectory, sitting at the high table surrounded by the monks who managed the various parts of the Abbey, its singing and bell-ringing, its kitchen and cellar, its infirmary and guest house. It was his birthday and he had invited them all to help him celebrate.

When the porter told him who was at the gate he laughed. 'Our good friend Richard of the Lea is welcome,' he said, 'whether he comes to pay his debt or no. Go fetch him hither.'

While the porter was away Sir Richard and Little John had been planning how they would tease the Abbot and make a fool of him. So when the porter returned, Sir Richard accompanied him into the refectory, and Little John followed close behind, bearing the bundle and the bag of gold. But when Sir Richard advanced towards the high table, Little John stayed behind the screen that shielded the high table from the draught, waiting to be called.

As he reached the table, Sir Richard fell on his knee and humbly bowed his head.

'Well, Sir Richard of the Lea,' said the Abbot roughly, 'you come in happy hour. Either to pay your debt or lose your land. Which is it to be?'

'My good Lord Abbot,' said Sir Richard. 'I crave a few months' grace. I have had ill luck. My corn is mildewed and my herds are sick. My friends desert me when I need them most. Give me till Easter, till that Holy time when Christ was crucified to pay the debts of all mankind.'

'Never a half-day more,' thundered the Abbot. 'The time to pay is now, the place is here.' And he struck the table with his huge fist, so that the silver goblets jumped into the air and made great splashes of wine when they came down. 'Your land, your castle, cattle, all belong to us.'

'Even his wife?' sniggered the Prior, and all the rest joined in the joke.

'Yet hear a word from the good squire who serves me,' said Sir Richard. 'He is a noble fellow. He will go surety for me, with his life. I beg you let him plead!' And with that he walked back to the screen, leaving the Abbot and the monks still laughing at the Prior's joke.

Behind the screen Little John had now unpacked the bundle and laid out the rich cloak and tunic and the jewelled belt and sword.

'Go, keep their laughter bubbling till I call,' whispered Sir Richard, pushing Little John into the refectory while he began to rip off his own tattered garments and dress himself in the handsome new ones.

When the Abbot and monks saw Little John they laughed louder than ever. 'A bearded oak tree for a squire,' roared the Abbot. 'A very giant!'

'Carries both horse and master on his shoulders!' shouted one of the monks.

'To save its hooves!' said another, and the whole room rocked with laughter again.

'You do me wrong, Lord Abbot,' said Little John. 'You wrong my master too. He comes in Christian charity. He begs a boon. Our Lord upon the cross showed pity, even to a thief. As men of God, can you deny the Lord who bore your sins and offers you your hope of bliss?'

'Enough! Enough!' shouted the Abbot. 'Try not to teach your betters but begone, back where you came from! And take your master with you. He broke his pledge. He failed to pay his debt. His land, his castle, all are ours.' And he slapped his great belly and took a long swig of wine, enjoying to the full his moment of triumph.

But even as he wiped his lips with his napkin Sir Richard

moved out from behind the screen in his glorious new clothes, every inch a nobleman, holding out the bag of gold. Suddenly there was silence throughout the hall. 'Enough! The game is played,' shouted Sir Richard. 'Come, John, and give our Christian friend his due!'

At this Little John strode across and took the leather bag. Then, returning to the Abbot's table, he poured the gold all over it, four hundred pounds in nobles. Some fell into the Abbot's lap, some hit the candlesticks, some rolled under the table amongst the sandalled feet, and one even fell into the Prior's soup, bounced up and hit him in the eye. Suddenly there was gold all over the place. The room was glittering with it, gold was everywhere. And when the ring and clatter had died down Sir Richard spoke.

'There, my Lord Abbot is the money due, under my bond. If, when you count it I have given short measure, you know my name and title. You know my castle home. You and your

43

monks befoul your habits and the Holy Name you bear. Your every action spits on the Lord as he was spat on long ago. But his tormentors he forgave, as I do you.'

With that he turned and made his way back to the gate, and Little John followed, picking up the torn and ragged clothes that he had left on the floor behind the screen. These he thrust into the arms of the porter. 'Give your good Abbot these,' he said, 'to remind him of the day Sir Richard of the Lea returned to pay his debt and win his lands again.'

*   *   *   *

A year later to the very day, Sir Richard came riding into the greenwood to pay back the money he had borrowed. He rode a fine piebald charger and behind him came a wagon loaded to the raves with bows and bowstrings and fine leather quivers, a hundred of each.

'Good Robin Hood,' he said as he dismounted, 'I come to pay four hundred pounds, borrowed a year ago this very day.' And he handed Robin a leather bag full of golden nobles.

'And what is more,' he went on, 'my wife in gratitude has sent a gift more useful far than gold. A hundred bows of finest yew with bowstrings twisted by herself and her maids, and a hundred leather quivers, to celebrate the noble deed you and your henchman Little John performed a year ago.'

'I accept your lady's gift with all my heart,' said Robin, pulling one of the bows from the wagon and testing it for weight and balance and the strength of its spring. 'Good bows are hard to come by. But I must refuse your gold.'

He went on to explain that only a few weeks beforehand Much and Will Scarlet had captured a monk riding from St Mary's Abbey to London and had brought him back to dine in the greenwood. When they asked him how much money he carried, he said he carried none. But when they stripped him of his habit they found he was wearing a padded corset with eight hundred pounds stitched inside it.

At first he pretended he had not known it was there. He made out that it belonged to the Abbot who had strained his back while hunting and wore it to support him. He himself had only borrowed it.

'Keep the support and we will keep the gold,' Robin had said, as Much unlaced the corset and tipped the shining coins out on the ground. 'Now go in peace and tell your Abbot that the Holy Virgin whose name his Abbey bears has paid Sir Richard's debt twice over. If you had told the truth she need have paid it only once. But she will understand.' Then they had taken the monk back to the highway and set him on his horse and sent him packing.

Sir Richard smiled and clasped Robin's hand. He had already learned from bitter experience that great churchmen whose duty it is to be pure and holy can often be selfish and cruel. He now learned that outlaws, who were supposed to be savage and lawless, could be noble and generous. It was a lesson he never forgot and he told Robin that if ever he or his men were in danger they could always come into his castle and he would help them against their foes. And so he bade them farewell and mounted his charger and rode away.

SOME people pretend that Robin never really existed, that his story is only a fairy tale like Tom Hickathrift or Jack the Giant killer. But for hundreds of years people said the same thing about King Arthur and his knights and about the famous Greek hero Odysseus and his long homecoming from the Trojan wars. Nowadays people believe that King Arthur and Odysseus really did exist, only they were such remarkable men that the stories of their lives lived on after they were dead and fresh adventures were added to their real ones – adventures they might have had and that people were ready to believe they really had had. This did not make them or their stories any less true but rather more so. And that is how it happened with Robin. The common people clung to his story and would not let it die. That is why it is just as much alive today as ever it was. And that is why I must tell you briefly where I believe it fits into our history, what England was like in those far-off days and why Robin and hundreds like him were forced to become outlaws.

You remember I told you that Hartoft was a very ancient place and that people had lived there on and off for thousands of years, in small family groups and later in tribes, until in the end, the whole of England was conquered by the Romans. But when Rome itself was attacked by the barbarians, her soldiers were called home to defend their motherland, leaving England to the mercy, first of the Saxons who sailed across from the western coast of Germany, and then of the Vikings, the greatest sailors the world has ever seen, who came from Norway in their famous dragon-ships.

But these Saxons and Vikings came not only to kill and burn and plunder, but to make their homes in the places they conquered, to marry local girls and have families by them, and to worship Jesus Christ instead of heathen gods like Woden, Odin and Thor. In England they even hammered out a fresh language, which we call Anglo-Saxon, and used it for writing exciting stories and beautiful poetry.

We shall never know how Anglo-Saxon England might have developed because it was suddenly torn apart by William the Conqueror, who came over from France in 1066 and beat the Anglo-Saxon army at the famous Battle of Hastings. William and his followers brought with them new laws, new customs and, what is more important, a new language. For instead of Anglo-Saxon, they spoke Norman French, and were still speaking it more than a hundred years later when King Richard, later called the Lionheart, came to the throne. Now no sooner was Richard crowned than he gathered an army and a great fleet of ships and went off to the Holy Land to help win back Jerusalem from the Saracens, leaving England to be governed by the Archbishop of Canterbury. He also left behind his cruel, ambitious and unpredictable brother Prince John. And it was

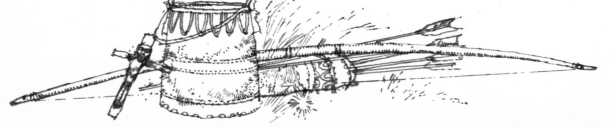

soon after Richard's fleet had sailed that Robin and Tricket escaped from Hartoft – only a few weeks before Robin's nineteenth birthday.

At this time there were no such things as maps so nobody had any idea what shape England really was. Even educated people thought the world was square with Jerusalem in the middle and England in the bottom left-hand corner. All they were really sure about was east and west, from the rising and setting of the sun. There were no signposts and villages were few and far between and very small, just farmhouses with a few huts clustered round them and tiny churches made of wood; and there were only two million people in the whole of England, instead of forty-six millions as there are today. The only proper roads were the ones built long ago by the Romans, but the country was criss-crossed by paths and tracks leading from village to village and from farm to farm, and to working places like coal and iron and lead mines, and sheepfolds and stone quarries and salt pans and charcoal-burners' huts.

Most houses were made of wood, because the stonemasons were all hard at work building castles and cathedrals and monasteries. The homes of the working people were rough thatched hovels with earth floors and hardly any furniture. They had neither windows nor chimneys and the whole family slept on the floor. And there were castles all over the country, hundreds of them, all full of savage soldiers ready to ride out and start killing each other.

But the thing you would have noticed most was that nearly half the country was covered with thick forests full of deer and wild boar and all manner of birds and fish. Until William the Conqueror came and captured the whole country, these forests belonged more or less to everyone and you could go into them without special permission. But William and his men were mad on hunting and wanted to keep the forests to themselves. So they made harsh laws to keep the forests private, and they employed foresters and verderers to look out for poachers and to stop people chopping down trees for firewood or to mend their houses. If people broke these laws they would be brought up in front of a special court and might have their hands cut off or their eyes put out or even be hanged. And if you were caught with a dog as Robin had been, it could have its front paws chopped off. Then it could never go hunting again. So now you can see how lucky Tricket had been to escape. But now we must get back to our story.

CHAPTER SIX

Alan a'Dale

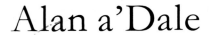

ONE summer's day Robin had been across to the little cave at Papplewick, where he kept a pair of fine horses always ready, to help him escape from danger or carry a message quickly from one part of the forest to another. They were cared for by a charcoal-burner named Luke Farthing and his son Peter, who worked in the woods nearby. Luke knew that most of Robin's men had been forced to become outlaws through no fault of their own, so he was always ready to help them. And because Luke was so kind and helpful, his wife would often find a joint of venison hidden under the pile of logs outside their cottage door.

Robin and his men had many friends like Luke, not only in the villages but in Nottingham itself, a network of people ready to hide them from the Sheriff's men or give them a meal of rye bread and bean soup or a bundle of goose feathers for their arrows, or bind up their wounds or put patches on their worn-out shoes. And the outlaws would say thank you with a piece of venison or a nice fat trout or a brace of woodcock.

Robin was making his way quietly back through the forest when he suddenly heard someone playing a harp and singing a sad little song. So he moved into the trees and waited for the singer to come closer. At last a beautiful young man appeared dressed in pale blue and singing:

> 'Alack, alack and well-a-day,
> My love is lost for ever,
> And I shall hold her in my arms,
> Ah, never, never, never.'

As he sang the last line he plucked his harp with a deep throbbing sound and the tears poured down his cheeks.

Robin stepped out from amongst the trees and stood in the young man's path.

'Who are you?' he said. 'And why are you so unhappy?'

'My name,' said the young man, 'is Alan of Barnsdale, but I am called Alan a'Dale. For two years I have wooed a beautiful girl named Alice. Tomorrow we were to be married in the church at Papplewick. Her wedding dress was made and my father had given us a little cottage to live in. But suddenly a rich old widower, Sir Worley Crake, came to Alice's father and said he would give him a thousand pounds if he could marry her instead of me. And as Alice's father loves money more than anything in the world, he agreed: and tomorrow the Bishop himself is going to marry them. So I have lost my love for ever, and I shall die of grief.' And the tears poured down his cheeks, and he started singing his sorrowful song once again.

When he heard this story Robin was very angry, and there and then made up his mind to go to the wedding and help Alan get his sweetheart back.

So, early next morning he sent ten of his finest archers to the church, led by Will Scarlet and Jacob Hobbe, telling them to take their places in the little gallery opposite the altar, hiding their bows and arrows at their feet and pretending to be simple villagers who had come to the wedding. The ten men did as they were told, getting to the church in good time and climbing on tip-toe up the ladder into the gallery.

Soon the verger arrived, to light the candles and tidy up the altar, never thinking to look up at the gallery where the outlaws were hiding, quiet as mice.

Meanwhile Robin was planting twenty more of his men amongst the bushes that grew close to the church, some of them overhanging it. Adam Leech and Tom Bold even climbed up into the branches of the old yew tree facing the very porch so that they could take aim at anyone going in or coming out. Then, having given them orders to stay dead quiet, Robin entered the church, sat down on a stone bench just inside the door, struck a chord on his harp and began to sing. He wasn't a very good singer and he couldn't play the harp at all well, but he made up for that by putting his heart and soul into it, singing his thanks to the Virgin Mary for having watched over him and his men for so long and for having guided them out of so many dangers.

At last the congregation began to arrive; people from Sir Worley's estate, villagers who had known Alice since she was a tiny girl, the verger's wife with Luke Farthing and his crippled sister hobbling along on crutches, and a few others who had heard there was going to be a wedding and who didn't want to miss it. They saw Robin's men standing or kneeling against the gallery rail but didn't notice their bows and quivers lying on the floor in front of them. They thought they were simple villagers like themselves.

Then came Little John and Friar Tuck with Alan a'Dale

49

between them, pushing their way through to the very front till they stood only a couple of yards from the altar, waiting for Robin's plan to start working.

Next came the Bishop and his Chaplain, both dressed in their church robes, the Bishop shining in his white embroidered cloak and looking very important in his episcopal hat and carrying a richly jewelled crook. All bishops carry one of those because they are supposed to be God's shepherds on earth, looking after the great flock of men and women who have lost their way and need help and guidance which only the church can give. But this particular Bishop had forgotten all about that. He was fat and red-faced and angry-looking and his eyes were blood-shot and you could see that he thought he was one of the most important people in the world. As he entered the church he paused, looking very angry, especially when Robin did not stop singing.

'Now fellow,' he said. 'Who gave you permission to sing and play in the House of the Lord?'

'I sing only of God's mother,' said Robin. 'Begging her to help all mankind in this troubled world and bring us safely into heaven when we die. It is an old song that I learned as a child. It is a kind of prayer.'

'If it is truly a prayer,' said the Bishop, 'you may continue. Indeed you may follow me and sing from the altar as I join these loving souls in holy matrimony.'

So the Bishop and his Chaplain moved through the congregation towards the altar and Robin followed close behind. Up till now there had been a lively buzz of conversation, but as the Bishop moved through the church, people stopped whispering and all was quiet.

Following the Bishop came a thin man with a little grey beard. He was only fifty-seven years old but he looked more like seventy. This was the bridegroom, Sir Worley Crake. He was finely dressed and was smiling a wintry smile, happy to be marrying such a young and beautiful wife and looking forward to taking her back to his home at Crakeforth. At his side walked his best man, Marmoset Bendix.

Sir Worley knew that the world was a dangerous place. He also knew there had been many whispers against him for marrying a young and lovely girl like Alice when it was well known that she loved Alan a'Dale. So to make sure nothing went wrong he had brought six archers with him, posting two of them outside the church and four just inside.

Lastly came Alice on her father's arm. She looked very pale and unhappy and her lip was trembling as if she was about to burst into tears. But she knew there was nothing she could do to change matters, so she was determined to put a brave face on it. Sir Worley gave her a wisp of a smile and she smiled bravely

51

back at him. And there they stood facing the altar; the best man, Sir Worley, then Alice and her father. And standing in the front row only a few feet away from them, Friar Tuck, Little John and the young man she so dearly loved, the man to whom she had long since given her heart, Alan a'Dale.

When all was quiet, the Bishop stepped forward. 'In the name of the Father, Son and Holy Ghost,' he said, 'we are met together to join this loving couple in Holy Matrimony according to the word of God.' He had a deep voice and he looked very determined. But before he could continue, Robin, who had been sitting on a little stool beside the altar, suddenly stood up and stepped forward.

'Tarry a moment,' he said in a ringing voice. 'Springtime should never wed with winter.' Then, pointing to Sir Worley, he said, 'This fellow is too old by far.'

'Back to your place!' roared the Bishop. 'How dare you interrupt!'

'Without true love between the partners,' said Robin, 'marriage is a sin against the Holy Ghost. It is a blasphemy.' Then, pointing at Sir Worley and Alice, 'This man is ready for the grave. The bride is as fresh as primrose in the dew.'

At this, the Bishop shouted to the archers, 'Men, take this fellow out.' But he was too late. Even as they moved, ten men were standing at the gallery rail with bows bent and arrows laid on the bow-strings.

'If your men move,' said Robin, 'they will die. And so will you.' Then shouting up to the gallery, 'Aim for their hearts, men. If they are marked to die, let their deaths be quick and painless.'

When they heard this, Sir Worley's archers laid down their bows and stepped back. Then Robin turned to Little John, 'Silence this noisy Bishop, John,' he said, and Little John needed no second command. Leaping on to the altar steps, he wrenched the silken cord from round the Bishop's waist, forced him roaring on to his knees and tied his hands tightly together. Then, snatching a napkin from the altar he rolled it up and stuffed it into his mouth, then turned him over on his face and sat on him.

By this time the congregation had begun to bubble with laughter. Certainly no-one lifted a finger to help the Bishop. Besides, they had now seen the row of archers in the gallery and had no wish to interfere. And all this time Alice and her father stood amazed, unable to believe what was happening. It was more like a dream than something real.

'Now,' said Robin to Sir Worley, 'your best place is back at home, with bedsocks and a nightcap and a bowl of gruel. Leave the girls to the boys. Get moving and be happy to escape alive.'

Sir Worley needed no second telling. Taking his best man by

the arm he made for the door, gathering his four archers on the way and was soon gone. Now the congregation were really laughing. They had come feeling sad that Alice was being forced to marry an old crock like Sir Worley. But when Robin stepped forward and said that such a marriage was wrong, and then, when Little John up-ended the Bishop and stuffed his mouth full of napkin and sat on him, and then when Robin told Sir Worley to go home to bed, the whole church began to overflow with joy. This was something they all understood and agreed with. Now at last Robin spoke to Alice.

'Young woman,' he said. 'Turn and look around. We know you had no wish to marry the old fellow I have just sent home to bed. But can you see anyone in all this company that you would like to marry?'

As he spoke he beckoned Alan to come a little closer. So when Alice turned round, there he stood with open arms, waiting for her to come to him. She needed no telling. With a wild cry she flew into his arms and he was holding her close and kissing her and stroking her golden hair. And all the people were shouting and laughing and crying until the little church itself seemed to be rocking with enjoyment.

But there was still one thing more to be done. Alice and Alan must be properly married. And who better to marry them than Friar Tuck, who now trundled up the altar steps and turned round to face the people.

'Friends,' he said. 'You know well that a man and a maid may not marry until warning has been given to the whole Parish, so that anyone who is against such a marriage may stand up and speak in public. And usually this is done three times, one Sunday after another. But I am giving the warnings now, all together, not only three but seven for good measure.' Then he shouted seven times running, 'If anyone here can tell us why these two children of God should not be joined together in marriage, let him speak up or keep his peace for ever.' Seven times he shouted it, so loudly that you could almost have heard it nine miles away in Nottingham. And each time the people shouted, 'No, get on and marry them,' and everybody was laughing and clapping and it was more like a fairground than a church.

Then Alan remembered that he had no ring. But an old lady standing near the front called out, 'Take mine. My man died twenty years ago. I am now in my ninetieth year. If he were still alive I know he would wish this child to have the ring with which he wed me seventy years ago.'

So Alice and Alan were married in the church at Papplewick in the heart of Sherwood Forest. The ancient church fell to the ground long ago and a new one was built on the spot. But the place is the same and under the ground are the foundations of the earlier church, the one Robin knew. And many of the trees surrounding the church are the great-great-grandchildren of the trees that were growing and blowing when Alan a'Dale married Alice and took her back to the greenwood.

But now there was no time for rejoicing. Sir Worley was already on his way into Nottingham to tell the Sheriff what had happened and get him to bring out his men. So Little John untied the Bishop and took the gag out of his mouth and bundled him and his Chaplain into their wagon and Robin's men came down from the gallery and the people began to go to their homes laughing with joy at what they had seen and heard. And the outlaws came down from the trees and Robin gave the old verger a golden noble for a present, the first one the old chap had ever seen, and the only one he ever did see.

So when the Sheriff and Sir Worley arrived with a hundred archers the church was empty and the door was shut and the little old verger was hiding behind one of the gravestones in the churchyard, laughing until the tears ran down his face to see them all so busy and so angry, finding nothing except the crumpled napkin which Little John had stuffed into the Bishop's mouth, lying where he had thrown it at the foot of the altar.

Meanwhile Alan and Alice were already miles away in the forest with Robin and his men.

CHAPTER SEVEN

The Green Stag

ABOUT a year after Robin came to the greenwood, the Sheriff of Nottingham decided to hold an archery contest, and bowmen came to try their skill from all the villages around; from Sibthorpe, Ilkeston, Bottesford, Ossington, Costock, Calverton, Spondon, Budby, Bingham and Hirthwaite and many others. And Little John brought a private team made up of himself and Luke Fletcher and Adam Leech and they called themselves the Barnsdale Boys.

It was a beautiful autumn day and crowds had gathered to enjoy the fun and cheer on their favourites. Carpenters had built a pavilion along one side of the shooting range, which was just outside the castle walls. And high up in the pavilion was a platform for the Sheriff and his wife and all their rich friends, so that they could have a clear view without having to mix with the common people.

The contest was so arranged that every team shot against every other team, and each archer had twelve shots at the target which was circular like a big flat canvas bag filled with straw and painted with different coloured rings to mark how many points you could get. And in the middle was a small circle painted gold which counted most points of all; so, of course, that was where every archer aimed to hit.

The shooting went on for the whole day and in the end only two teams were left, the one from Ossington and the Barnsdale Boys who said they had come down from the north especially to beat the archers of Nottingham.

There was great excitement as the two teams lined up for the final shoot-off. First Ossington took the lead, then the Barnsdale Boys, then it was Ossington again with their leader, Tom Colle, hitting the gold circle seven times with his twelve shots, putting Ossington well in front. And my, how the people cheered! Now Ossington must surely take the prize. Luke and Adam had both shot quite well, but when the judges added up the score it meant that Little John would have to hit the gold nine times if the Barnsdale Boys were to win.

Now the crowd was hushed. Was it possible that this great bearded Yorkshireman who had shot so well all the afternoon but who had never hit the gold more than seven times could now hit it nine times out of twelve? They doubted it. And so did Little John himself.

But John was one of those people who always do best when things are hardest, the kind who always rise to the occasion, and this time he rose to it like a giant. So rapidly did he shoot that he scarcely seemed to aim. First shot a gold. Second shot a gold. A gold for third. Now the crowd were yelling and the Sheriff and his friends in the grandstand were on their feet clapping and waving their scarves and shouting, 'Well shot, Barnsdale!'

But that was nothing to the shout that went up as the next four arrows joined the first three. Now it needed only two more golds to beat the team from Ossington. But there was a groan as the next two shots went wide. Only by half an inch or so but that half inch was half an inch too much. Now John had only

three arrows left and if Barnsdale were to win, two of them must be planted in the gold.

He made no mistake with his first shot. Straight and true it sped, bang in the middle. Still he had only two shots left and one of them would have to be a gold if Barnsdale were to win. And would you believe it the next shot missed! Only by a hair's breadth but when the judges came to examine the target they found a thread of red canvas between the arrow and the edge of the gold circle. 'A miss! A miss!' shouted the Herald and the crowd groaned. Now John had only one arrow left and Barnsdale needed one more gold to win!

John was very calm. He had been shooting on and off for nearly five hours, but his massive shoulders and powerful arms felt as loose as when he started, and he smiled as he stroked his mighty bow and prepared for the final shot. Once more the crowd were hushed. The arrow was laid upon the string, the bow pushed forward nearly to its head and then released. Next moment it was quivering among the other eight in the centre of the target. A final roar went up from the crowd. Little John had scored nine golds, the Barnsdale Boys had won!

Standing with his wife and wealthy friends the Sheriff shouted, 'Well shot Barnsdale!' and told one of his servants to bring the winning team up into the grandstand so that he could shake them by the hand. And when Little John stood before him, with Luke and Adam just behind, the Sheriff said he had never seen such shooting and he thanked them for giving Nottingham such a fine day's sport.

'Tell me your name, my friend, and where you come from,' he said. 'Men call me Reynold Greenleaf,' said Little John. 'I hail from Doncaster, my mates from further north. We heard of your match and came to try our luck.'

'How would you like to stay in Nottingham and work for me?' asked the Sheriff. 'I need a Captain for my Bodyguard. You could be just the man.'

Little John turned to Luke and Adam. 'If my mates agree,' he said, 'I could think of nothing finer.' And he gave them a knowing wink.

'No need to ask your mates,' the Sheriff said. 'I am asking you, not them. The pay is good, the quarters warm and dry, and food the very best. Report this evening after supper at the castle gate and there my men will see you well bestowed.' So Little John took service with the Sheriff, sending Luke and Adam back into the forest to tell Robin that he now had a spy inside the enemy's camp!

When Robin heard this he arranged for Mark Tardiffe, who was very clever at disguising himself, to go and sit outside the castle gate pretending to be a poor ragged beggar; so that every few days, Little John could put a farthing in his begging bowl and whisper the latest news to him, such as when the Sheriff was planning to bring out a raiding party and how many soldiers he would be bringing and which parts of the forest they would be searching. And Mark would be able to hobble away into the forest and tell it all to Robin.

That same evening Little John reported at the castle gate and was shown his quarters leading off the guardroom, and one of the Sheriff's men brought him a fine supper on a tray and a jug of wine and laid his new uniform across a stool and everyone in the guardhouse saluted him and called him 'Captain Greenleaf'. After the hard life of the forest this just suited Little John and he settled into his new life as if he had been born to it, swaggering in new livery and rattling out orders like a machine gun.

The Sheriff congratulated himself on having found such a fine strong fellow to serve him, and his wife imagined how wonderful it would be to feel those strong arms around her and that tall powerful body lying beside her instead of having to sleep with her fat and ugly husband who usually came to bed half-drunk and lay all night snoring.

Every few days Mark carried messages back to Robin, warning him whenever he needed to be specially watchful. And whenever the Sheriff took a raiding party into the forest, John would always guide them away from Robin's secret hiding places, and especially from the entrance to the cave where the Sheriff and his men could often have found fifty or sixty men making new bows and winding new bowstrings or patching their garments with leather and bits of different coloured cloth or fastening steel points to their arrows and fixing little slips of goose feather to the other ends to make them fly straight and true.

Little John spent nearly a year as Captain of the Sheriff's Bodyguard, and he was the most popular person in the castle, always good-tempered and always ready to use his great strength to help others. Only one man disliked him and that was the cook. Up till now, he had been the Sheriff's favourite because he could make such wonderful dishes and serve them up so tastily. But now the Sheriff and his lady seemed able to talk of no-one but Reynold Greenleaf. In fact it was 'Greenleaf this' and 'Greenleaf that' from morning till night, and this made the cook so jealous that he went out of his way to be rude to Little John, giving him the worst pieces of meat for his rations, and the cheapest wine, and bread so stale that it was full of maggots. Until at last Little John decided to teach him a lesson. And this is how he did it.

When the Sheriff arranged his next hunting party John pretended to have a fever and asked if he could stay behind for once, he felt so ill. And the Sheriff agreed. His men were now so well trained he felt sure they could manage for once without their tall, bearded Captain.

The Sheriff and his men set off for the forest with a great clattering of hooves and sounding of horns, leaving John waiting until they were well clear of the city and deep into the forest. Then he got up and dressed and went down into the kitchen where he found the cook and the steward busy washing up the dinner things.

'For months you have served me stinking meat and sour wine and bread fit only for pigs,' said Little John. 'Now make me the sort of dinner I deserve, and the sort I mean to have.'

Of course the cook and the steward didn't like being spoken to like that, even by the Captain of the Sheriff's bodyguard, and at first they took no notice of him but went on working as if nothing had happened. So Little John asked again, this time shouting so loud that even the cook couldn't go on pretending he hadn't heard.

'Dinner was served an hour ago,' he said. 'Now we have washing-up to do. There's bread and cheese in the cupboard and you are welcome to a mug of ale. Take some of that and get back to your guardroom.'

'No bread and cheese for me, you rascal,' said Little John. 'The pantry is full to bursting with good fare. Go fetch me what I ask and make it hot.'

'I'll fetch you something hotter still,' said the cook, lifting a frying pan and brandishing it like an axe. John did not wait for it to fall. He thrust out a leg and neatly tripped the cook, then stooped down and lifted him bodily into the air and dropped him into the sink amongst the boiling water and dirty dishes. The cook screamed as he tried in vain to clamber out of the hot water, and John roared with laughter to see him kicking about among the steaming pots and pans. But he had forgotten the steward who had crept round the table carrying a vast rolling pin which he suddenly lifted and brought down with a thwack on Little John's head. If Little John had not rolled under the table as he fell, thus giving himself time to recover, that might have been the end of the fight. When he did recover and when he crawled out into the open he was very angry, and when Little John was angry you could be sure the fur would fly.

It would take too long to describe all the details of the fight that followed. The cook, streaming wet, managed to scramble out of the sink and grab his broadsword from behind the kitchen door, while the steward still brandished the rolling pin. But in a flash Little John seized the fireguard and a long iron poker, using the one as a shield and the other as a weapon. And so they battled to and fro and the kitchen rang with their shouting and with the sound of iron on iron and the smashing of chairs and crockery. At last, getting both cook and steward pinned into a corner and holding them there with the fireguard, John reached out and hauled the kitchen table towards him. The cook and steward tried to jump clear, but in their eagerness to get away they fell on top of one another. Now was John's chance. Hurling poker and fireguard aside he upturned the table and brought it down on top of his two victims who lay underneath five hundredweight of beech and oak. Then he jumped on to the upturned table, adding his own weight to the load.

'Now will you get me some dinner?' he said, speaking to the cook's head, which was the only part of him you could now see.

'No,' said the cook. So John started jumping up and down on the table, putting all his weight into it.

'Now will you get me some dinner?' he said again.

'No,' said the cook, not so boldly this time, as he felt the weight of the table with Little John's added to it.

So Little John started jumping up and down once more. 'Now will you get me some dinner?' he said. There was a long pause and then, just as John was about to start jumping once more, 'Yes,' said the cook.

When Little John lifted the table up and set the cook and steward free they were more than ready to do his bidding and soon laid a fine feast on the table, woodcock pie and roast ribs of pork, with venison pastie and fish collops and partridge, and a flagon of red wine, and a fine Yorkshire cheese to finish off with. Then, pausing between one bite of venison pastie and the next, Little John said something that surprised them. 'Why not sit down and share the feast? Here is enough for all three of us.'

Then he began to laugh and his laugh was so warm and rich and friendly that the cook and the steward started laughing too, in spite of their bruises. And they pulled up their stools and joined him.

'Don't tell me you like this rotten Sheriff?' said John.

'Surely we do not,' said the cook. 'He is hard and cruel and his wife is proud and greedy. But a man must work, to eat and keep his family. If I were young again I would join Robin Hood and his merry men in the greenwood.'

'And so would I,' said the steward.

'But they are bandits and robbers,' said Little John. 'They have been put outside the law. A man can kill them and not be punished for it. They are outlaws.'

'I know that,' replied the cook. 'But the law was made for the rich and the men who enforce it are mostly cruel and stupid and selfish. They have no care for true justice and no thought for the poor. So it is often better to be outside the law than in its crooked arms. If Robin or one of his men were with us at this moment I would take the greenwood oath and join his band.'

'And so would I,' said the steward.

'Then join it now,' said Little John. 'I am his right-hand man. I am not Reynold Greenleaf as I have pretended this last year, but Little John of Hathersage. I am sick to death of serving this cruel Sheriff and his ugly dame. I am returning to the greenwood this very day. You are welcome to come with me. We have need of brave hearts and strong arms.'

Then they all began to laugh till the tears rolled down their cheeks and fell on to their venison pasties and they stood and swilled great draughts of the Sheriff's finest wine and hugged each other as if they were already brothers.

'Let us not go empty handed,' said the cook. 'Let us relieve our master of a few pieces of his precious table ware. A few golden plates and a silver flagon or two.' 'Yea,' said the steward. 'I will go fetch the little hand cart and we will load it till it creaks.'

So the cook unlocked the strong room and took out silver jugs and tankards and serving dishes and candlesticks, together with ivory-handled knives and golden sweetmeat boxes; and

when the steward came back with the handcart they loaded it up with the Sheriff's treasures and covered the whole thing with an old embroidered tablecloth.

Then they set out for the castle gate, Little John and the cook walking in front and the steward pushing the cart. Seeing the Captain of the Sheriff's Bodyguard in the lead, the gatekeeper let them through without question, and soon they were pushing the cart along one of the forest paths which Little John knew so well. Suddenly they heard the sound of horns and the barking of dogs and realised that the Sheriff and his huntsmen were coming towards them. Little John had to think fast.

Swiftly pushing the cart into a hollow sheltered by thick bushes and telling the cook and the steward to keep dead quiet until he returned, he hurried on towards the noise of the hunting. As it drew nearer he started to run.

At last there was the Sheriff on his horse and the huntsmen riding behind him and the hounds spread out in front searching for the scent. Seeing Little John, the Sheriff reined in his horse and stopped.

'Now Greenleaf,' he said. 'What brings you here? You said you had a fever and must stay a-bed.'

'Yes, Your Honour,' said Little John. 'But after dinner I felt stronger, and I remembered it was my duty to be always at your side in case of need. So I arose and hurried here to join you. And glad I am that I did so, for I have just seen a wonderful sight. A huge stag with noble head and mighty horns and body all of green.'

'A giant stag all green!' said the Sheriff. 'You must be mad!'

'I promise you I saw it, feeding quietly in a glade. Follow me and I will lead you to it. I swear that no such creature was ever seen in Sherwood, and the honour of killing it must be yours. But you must come alone. It is a magic beast and the sound of horse and hound will drive it off before we reach its lair. Surely 'tis something never seen before. Trust me to guide you safely.'

So the Sheriff gathered his men together and they called in the hounds and the huntsmen put them on the leash and the Sheriff and Little John went on together to find the great green stag and bring it down, the Sheriff riding his horse and Little John walking beside him.

On and on they went, deeper and deeper into the forest, until the Sheriff began to suspect he was being led into a trap. Even if he tried he would never find his way back, for they were now too far from the rest of the hunt. Besides it was beginning to grow dark.

At last they came to a long uphill slope ending in a steep cliff, a mixture of sand and stone, and there in the open space below them a camp fire was burning and over the fire a huge cauldron hanging from a tripod, and round the fire thirty or forty men eating their evening meal.

One of the men was tall and slim and bronzed and handsome. Another, massive with muscle, was dressed as a friar. A third was short and wiry and walked with a limp. The men were dressed in green with hoods of reddish brown, and stacked against a tree were their bows and quivers, and their swordbelts lay around or hung from broken branches. And in the midst was a young man with a ladle, serving them broth from the cauldron while the friar carved great slices of pork and venison at a rough side table loaded with fine food and Alice was pouring wine from a silver flagon.

'This,' said Little John, 'is the secret haunt of the green stag, and there in the midst stands the stag himself. His name is Robin Hood. On his behalf I bid you welcome.' Then he gave the Sheriff a push which sent him headlong over the cliff, bouncing down between the rocks and finally rolling right into the middle of the supper party.

'I bring you a guest,' shouted Little John, 'Our friend the Sheriff. He greets you all and you must bid him welcome in a

64

loving cup.' Then he took the Sheriff's horse by its bridle and began to lead it downwards by a gentler path.

The outlaws roared with laughter when they saw the Sheriff come tumbling down the cliff and when he came to rest they picked him up and helped to dust him down. Then, as he stood there, panting and bewildered, Robin stepped forward.

'Welcome, good Sheriff, to our humble board. We live the simple life but the food is plentiful and finely cooked.' The Sheriff was so angry at the trick Little John had played on him that he could hardly speak. He stood in the midst of the outlaws red-faced and spluttering with rage. But at last a place was laid for him at the long table next to Robin and he sat down.

By this time Little John had tethered the Sheriff's horse and joined the throng at table.

'His Worship wishes to spend the night with us,' he said. 'He is eager to sample life in the greenwood at least once before he dies.'

Then he went back to find the cook and steward and help them bring their handcart out of its hiding place. He found them waiting patiently for his return and soon led them into a little clearing close to the camp. There they unloaded the Sheriff's treasures and carried them into the corner of the cave where they did the cooking.

'A plate of venison and a cup of wine for our new recruit,' said Robin as he handed the Sheriff one of his own silver plates, chased round the edges with hunting scenes and with his coat of arms engraved in the centre, and one of his own precious goblets, its stem encrusted with amethysts and rubies.

When the Sheriff received his supper on one of his own plates and was offered wine in one of his own goblets, he could hardly believe his eyes and once more he began to make funny spluttering noises as if he was going to burst. And the more angry he became the more the outlaws laughed. Only Robin behaved as if nothing strange had happened, now helping the Sheriff to a nice piece of lean, now carving him a choice morsel of fat, now filling his goblet with wine, then helping him to wipe his mouth and beard with a napkin, like a mother tending her favourite child.

When everyone had finished eating Robin stood up and made a speech.

'This day,' he said, 'The Lord High Sheriff of Nottingham has honoured us with his presence. He has sat at our table and enjoyed an outlaw's supper. But that brings him only half way into our brotherhood. Now we must disrobe him top to toe and dress him in the costume of the greenwood, the garb of Robin Hood.' Then, to a group of outlaws sitting nearest to him, 'Pray help his Worship to undo his buttons.'

At this four or five men sitting nearest to the Sheriff raised

him to his feet and began undressing him, until he stood there in
his underclothes, shivering with cold. Then Alice went into the
cave and fetched a complete outfit; long woollen hose and well-
worn buckskin boots and leather jerkin, complete with belt and
dagger. And the outlaws dressed him up in it, then clapped a
red-brown hood and cape over his head and shoulders and put a
longbow into his hands and hung a quiver-full of arrows across
his shoulders, until he stood there in the glow of the camp fire,
every inch an outlaw. And Robin and his men gave a great cheer
as they stood round him, laughing and slapping him on the
back like old friends.

The Sheriff was furious at this undignified behaviour but
there was nothing he could do about it. So, when Friar Tuck
had said prayers and the night watch had gone to their look-out
posts high up in the trees, Will Stutely and Alan a'Dale led him
to his greenwood bed, which was in a little hollow between the
roots of a giant oak tree. And there he lay all night with a bundle
of moss for a pillow and a rough woollen cloak to keep him

warm. Tricket kept guard over him, baring her teeth and growling whenever he stirred or turned over in his sleep.

In the morning the Sheriff begged Robin to set him free and Robin agreed. 'But first,' he said, 'you must swear never to harm me or any of my men and never to attack us again. You must swear it by the Virgin Mary, the Mother of God Himself and call on all my men to be your witnesses.'

'Gladly,' said the Sheriff who had spent a cold and uncomfortable night and was in no mood to argue. 'Let your Friar say the words and I will speak them after him.'

So Friar Tuck stepped forward and spoke the words and the Sheriff repeated them, phrase by phrase.

'I, Wilfred, Sheriff of His Royal Majesty's City of Nottingham do hereby take my dying oath never forthwith to hurt or harry Robert Hood, known throughout the North Country as Robin, friend of the poor, helper of the weak and lover of freedom, or any of his noble band now resident in the Royal Forest of Sherwood. And I swear to do all in my power to plead for them with the King himself, showing that their cause is just and that they are good men and true, faithful to King and Country, only seeking justice and Christian charity towards all men. This I swear by Almighty God and by His Holy Mother the Blessed Virgin Mary, and if I break this oath may God strike me dead.' And all the outlaws crossed themselves and said 'Amen'.

'Now,' said Robin, 'you can depart. A horse awaits you and your old friend Reynold Greenleaf will lead you through the forest and set you on the road to Nottingham.'

Then they brought out a tired old horse and lifted the Sheriff into its saddle facing backwards, so that he should not remember the way he had come, and Little John led him to the margin of the forest where it meets the Great North Road. There for a moment they stopped. 'Thank you good Sheriff,' said Little John, 'for a very entertaining year. You must agree that Reynold Greenleaf served you well. But his heart was not really in the job. He hungered to be back with his friends in the greenwood. There he will drink your health in your own red wine from one of your own golden goblets. Fare you well.'

Then, turning the horse's head towards Nottingham, he gave it a kindly slap on its rump, and away it went at a trot, with the Sheriff still sitting back to front, a strong hempen cord binding him to its neck and his feet tied firmly under its belly.

Little John watched till horse and rider were well on their way. Then, waving them a cheery goodbye he made his way back to the camp to tell Robin and Friar Tuck and Much and Will Scarlet and Alan a'Dale and all the others what life was like in Nottingham castle, and how much he had missed them and how glad he was to be back.

CHAPTER EIGHT

Capture!

NOW that the Sheriff had sworn a solemn oath not to harm or harass the outlaws, Robin felt he could safely go into Nottingham to hear Mass at St Mary's, his favourite church, without bothering to dress up as someone else. For a long time now he had been forced to go in disguise, sometimes shaving his beard and the top of his head and wearing the white habit of a monk, sometimes pretending to be a blind beggar or a wounded soldier back from the wars and only able to walk on crutches, sometimes a pedlar or a shepherd. On one occasion he even dressed up as an old woman selling apples in the market place.

The outlaws had many friends in Nottingham and in the surrounding villages, people who would hide them from the Sheriff's men, either in cupboards or in their attics or amongst the barrels of ale in their cellars; or move them from house to house in the dark. On one occasion Robin was even wrapped in a woollen shroud and laid out on a friendly undertaker's slab, his face made deathly pale with a mixture of fuller's earth and water and his hands crossed on his chest, while the Sheriff's men searched for him all over the house. And he was not the only one who played such tricks. In the great cave they had a special disguising department full of old clothes, some tattered and torn, some fine enough for a lord or even a king; and eye patches and crutches and stuffing to push down their jerkins to give them pretended fat bellies, and rough beards made of horse hair mixed with wool, and charcoal and walnut juice and little pots of glue and a couple of broken looking-glasses. They would spend hours turning themselves into lords or lawyers or beggars or priests or soldiers or pedlars or cripples or halfwits, whatever their various plots and plans seemed to require.

Robin was the best. He could not only change what he looked like, he could change his voice as well, making it old or young, high-class or low-class, male or female, English or French. For in those far-off times most of the rich people spoke the French which William the Conqueror brought over with him when he won the Battle of Hastings, while the ordinary people were still speaking the language that had begun to grow up around King Alfred's time and had been used for writing beautiful poetry and exciting stories until William came and broke it all up. Friar Tuck even taught Robin to speak a little Latin, like the priests and monks spoke. He could say 'Pax vobiscum' and 'Ave Maria' and the whole of 'Pater noster qui est in coelis, sanctificetur nomen tuum,' which is Latin for 'Our Father which art in Heaven hallowed be Thy name.'

But now, trusting the Sheriff's oath, he could go to Mass as Robin Hood and no-one would harm him. Little John told him not to risk it, so did Friar Tuck, but Robin said, 'The Sheriff swore by our Lady. That oath is sacred. He who breaks it will go to Hell for all Eternity. He will not take that risk.

So one Sunday morning he went into Nottingham as himself, quite openly, greeting old friends as he passed along the narrow streets; friends who had helped him in time of need or warned him when the Sheriff was bringing soldiers into the forest. People thought it was strange that he should venture into the city undisguised, but knowing how brave and clever he was, they thought that perhaps this was just another trick he was playing. So he walked gaily along Woolpack Lane, turning left into Stoney Street and so into the tiny church.

The bell was ringing for Mass and as he crossed himself and knelt at the altar it was still ringing: and the Priest was repeating the wonderful promise made by Jesus to his disciples when they ate their little supper together not long before he was taken out and nailed to the cross. Never had Robin felt so happy or so secure. The Sheriff had sworn to give up hunting him and his comrades and had promised to ask the king that they might be brought back within the arms of the law where they felt they truly belonged. They had never been against the law, only against those people who twisted it out of shape and used it for their own cruel and selfish ends. Now perhaps things would be different. Of course, he was foolish to be so trusting. He should have listened to Little John and Friar Tuck. But he had not. He believed that an oath taken in the name of Jesus and his holy Mother was as sure as the rock upon which Nottingham castle itself was built, and that the sun shining through the window of the little church was a promise that from now on things were going to be different.

So when the priest handed him the morsel of bread and the cup of wine, his only thought was of Jesus and his holy Mother, who now sat in Heaven helping God to help men and women out of their troubles and bring true justice down to earth. He did not notice that the monk kneeling beside him at the altar had recognised him and had slipped out of the church to tell the

Sheriff and his officers that if they looked sharp they could capture the greatest outlaw in the land. For Robin had come without bow and arrows, armed only with his broadsword which he had unbuckled and laid at the steps of the altar before kneeling down.

But soon there came a great shouting and tramping of feet and twenty soldiers came thundering into the church. 'Where is this traitor?' they shouted. 'Where is this fellow who kills and robs and makes a mock of the law and of the great High Sheriff of Nottingham?'

In a flash Robin reached for his sword and drawing it from its sheath stood facing them. Then began a terrible battle, one man fighting against twenty. Holy images were knocked down and trampled on, the silver chalice was sent flying from the Priest's hand, and the people who had come to Mass fled in terror fearing for their lives.

Wild with anger that the Sheriff should have broken his oath so easily, Robin fought like a madman and soon the floor of the church was swimming with blood as he and the Sheriff's men fought. His only wish was to get to the space beneath the belfry and pull himself up to safety by the bell-rope hanging there. Seven men he slew before he came within reach of it and still there were thirteen slashing at him, trying to cut him down.

At last the rope was dangling in front of him and he leapt to catch hold of it and haul himself up, out of reach of his attackers. Making a strong loop for his left foot, he hung there swinging to and fro from the belfry, lashing and stabbing at the Sheriff's men below him and setting the church bell ringing loud and clear as if to wake the dead.

Five more he killed from his vantage point and would have killed them all if one crafty fellow had not climbed up the ladder and cut the bellrope with his dagger, letting Robin tumble down amongst his maddened foes, still clutching his end of the rope and swinging his broadsword like a man possessed.

But all to no avail, for now the Sheriff himself arrived along with the monk who had first recognised Robin as they knelt together at the altar, and a troop of archers who pulled their weary comrades out of the fight and formed a ring round the bottom of the tower with their bows bent and arrows pointed at Robin's heart.

'One more swing of your sword,' thundered the Sheriff, 'and you will be a dead man. You will have no time to confess your sins. You have murdered twelve of my finest men. You will go straight to Hell.'

All was suddenly quiet. Now it was a single blade against a dozen deadly bows and Robin was so weary he could scarcely lift his arms. If he moved he would be filled with arrows. It was better to give in than die. So, turning his bloodstained sword

around till he was holding the blade instead of the handle he advanced towards the Sheriff, offering it as a token of surrender.

'Now,' said the Sheriff as he took the sword, 'we shall get you under lock and key.' Then he put his arm round the monk's shoulder. 'And you, my good friend, shall have the honour of riding to London tomorrow, to tell Prince John that we have captured the greatest traitor in the land, one who steals the king's deer, insults his chosen magistrates and murders men on holy ground. Then the prince can choose whether Master Robin shall be hanged here in Nottingham or carted to London for a common show and hanged before the whole city.' And he laughed a cruel laugh as his men clapped chains on Robin's hands and feet and dragged him out of the church, through the waiting crowd and away to the castle where he was flung into Mortimer's Hole and fastened to one of the great iron rings in the wall.

But the Sheriff had forgotten that Robin had good friends in Nottingham, many of them crowding the church to see what would happen next. So, long before he had time to order the city gates to be locked and barred in case Robin's men should try to rescue him, a messenger had slipped away into the forest to tell the outlaws that their leader had been captured and was now imprisoned in the terrible dungeon underneath the castle: and that the monk who had betrayed him would be riding to London in the morning to carry the good news to Prince John and ask him where and when he would wish to see Robin hanged.

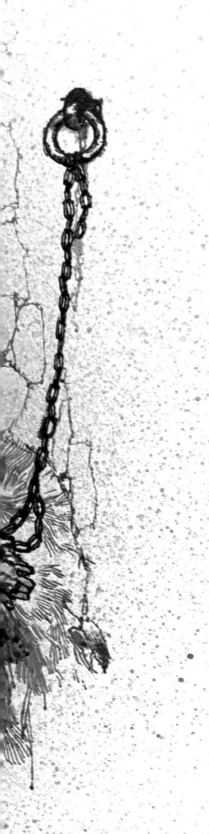

Next morning, soon after it was light, Little John and Much the miller's son with half-a-dozen tough companions, slipped out of camp and made their way to the edge of the forest where it borders the London road. There they lay hidden in the bushes waiting for the monk to come riding past.

Soon they heard the jingling of harness and the trotting of hooves and down the road came two horses, one carrying the monk, the other his servant, a fellow about twenty years old. The monk was singing as he came riding past. It was a great honour to be carrying a letter from the Sheriff of Nottingham to Prince John, the king's brother, especially as he had written the letter in his own handwriting. For after he had seen Robin thrown into the dungeon, the Sheriff had taken the monk up to his private chamber in one of the towers. There he had taken parchment and an ink horn and a new quill pen and had ordered the monk to write the following words as he spoke them:

'To His Royal Highness Prince John, Guardian of the Realm and of Lands Beyond the Seas, greeting from his humble and dutiful servant, Wilfred, Lord High Sheriff of Nottingham.

This day we have taken the foul outlaw and traitor Robin Hood who, in company with a hundred evil fellows whom he calls his Merry Men has robbed and done to death so many of His Majesty's loyal subjects hereabouts, has murdered monks and desecrated churches and worst of all has taken untold numbers of His Royal Majesty's Deer. Now he is safely guarded in our castle and we await your Royal pleasure whether to bring him to London for general show and public hanging or whether your Royal Highness will deign to honour us by bringing your Royal Person to Nottingham to be witness to his execution here.

Writ this day September 27th in the year of Our Lord eleven hundred and ninety-three and given under our seal.

Wilfred.'

The monk wrote in his finest hand and the parchment was duly folded and sealed and now he was on his way to London to meet Prince John in person and to place the letter in his hands. No wonder he was singing and no wonder he was surprised when a tall bearded fellow sprang out into the middle of the road and ordered him and his companion to turn their horses into the forest.

The bearded fellow was, of course, Little John and he was soon followed by Much and the half dozen others, all fully armed. The monk did as he was told, only venturing to ask why he had been stopped and how long his captors meant to keep him prisoner, to which the outlaws made no reply.

At last they reached a little clearing deep in the forest, where the monk and his companion were ordered to dismount. Only then did Little John answer.

'Yesterday,' he said, 'you betrayed our leader Robin Hood. And now you are riding to London to bring news of his capture to Prince John and to ask what death he shall suffer, and when and where.' Then, turning to Much, 'Open his saddle bag,' he said. The monk tried to protest but Much had already opened the leather satchel and found the Sheriff's letter and handed it to John.

Seizing the monk by the shoulders, John forced him to his knees. 'Now fellow,' he said, 'we are no scholars. We cannot read. We therefore command you to open this letter and spell it out to us. At once.' And he drew his huge sword and swung it close to the monk's head. At this the servant trembled and the monk turned deathly pale. I need not tell you that the monk obeyed, reading the letter in a voice filled with fear. When Little John heard what the Sheriff had written he laughed. 'My guess was right,' he said. 'But you are not the man to carry such a precious message. Stay on your knees and say your prayers. Your time is ripe for heaven, if they will have you there.'

The monk wept and pleaded for his life, but the outlaws had no pity for such people. This fellow was cruel and cunning. Because of him Robin was now in fearful danger, perhaps already dead. If they let him live he would betray more people.

So, having given him time to make his peace with God, the outlaws knocked him senseless with a block of wood, then dragged him into the bushes and hacked his head off. Then scooped out a shallow grave and thrust him into it. So much for treacherous monks!

Meanwhile the servant was also on his knees, praying hard and weeping, certain that his own end was near. But Little John lifted him up and comforted him. 'You need not fear,' he said. 'You had no hand in the plot to capture our beloved leader. All the same we cannot set you free till Much and I return from London. Our comrades here will lead you to our camp.'

'And if you care to take the greenwood oath, you can be one of us,' said Much. ''Tis worth considering!'

So the servant was led away into the forest while Little John and Much mounted the two fine horses and trotted southwards at a brisk canter with the Sheriff's letter tucked inside Little John's jerkin.

Now they had only one problem. The seal on the letter had been broken and would have to be mended before they could show it to the Prince's officers and pretend they were really and truly messengers from the Sheriff. For it was stamped with the Sheriff's badge on one side and a picture of the City of Nottingham on the other. But when they stopped to examine it they found that the seal had not been as badly broken as they feared. All it needed was a little warm beeswax to join the pieces together. Now all archers carried pieces of wax which they used to make their bow-strings waterproof, working it gently into the twisted flax. All they needed was a fire to soften the wax.

Turning into the forest once again they gathered some dry sticks, while Much took out his tinder box and struck the steel on the flint and Little John blew gently as the sparks fell on the fragments of dry linen at the bottom of the box. Soon a tiny flame spurted up and before long a fire was burning, fed by the dry sticks and odds and ends of broken branches lying around.

Waiting till the centre of the fire was smouldering red, Much warmed a piece of wax till it was almost melting, then pressed it into the seal with the point of his dagger until you would never know it had been broken. When it was cool they remounted their horses and rode on southwards.

CHAPTER NINE

Rescue!

AT last Little John and Much found themselves approaching London and, as they drew near, there was Westminster Abbey, Edward the Confessor's great church, its pale stone glistening in the sunshine, with masons and carpenters and blacksmiths still working on it, and barge-loads of fresh stone lying along the banks of the Thames, ready to be brought ashore and cut to shape. And sheets of lead being melted thin for roofing.

When John and Much asked where they might find Prince John, people looked at them in surprise, for they were still in their rough forest clothes and their horses were tired and stained with mud. At last a kindly old man pointed to a fine building not far away. 'There lies the palace,' he said, 'though I doubt if such as you will ever be admitted, even to the courtyard.'

But when Little John showed the letter and the seal, the guards let them pass without question and they soon found themselves in a little room next to the Presence Chamber, which was the most important room in the palace.

Here they waited till a servant put his head through the curtains and beckoned them into the main room. There, sitting on a throne was a short red-haired man, dressed in rich robes, glittering with jewels and wearing a slender golden crown with a single ruby fastened to its front. He was eating fresh peaches and spitting the stones out on to the floor, then taking swigs of wine from a golden goblet which a servant kept filling from a huge flagon. His eyes moved restlessly to and fro as he ate and drank and every now and then he laughed to himself as if he had just thought of something funny. Around him stood his courtiers rather nervously. This was Prince John, brother of Richard the Lionheart who, as I told you at the beginning, had gone off to the Holy Land to win back Jerusalem from the Saracens, leaving his young brother to help rule the country while he was away.

When he saw Little John and Much, the Prince was so surprised that some of the wine went down the wrong way and he nearly choked. But the Chamberlain slapped him on the back and wiped the wine off the front of his gown with a clean napkin, so he soon recovered. 'Who in the name of God are you?' he spluttered. 'And why has my Chamberlain allowed you into my presence?'

'We come from the Lord High Sheriff of Nottingham,' said Little John. 'And we bring news that will gladden your Royal Highness's heart. We travelled roughly dressed for fear of outlaws on the road. They rob the rich. Poor men they leave in peace.' And he went down on one knee and handed the Prince the Sheriff's letter.

Prince John tore open the seal and read the letter aloud to the whole court and one could see from the cruel gleam in his eye that Robin's fate was already settled. 'What think you gentlemen?' he said. 'Shall we hang this fellow here or make a progress to the north, to give our people there a good day's sport?' Then, not waiting for an answer, he said, 'Let's have him here in Smithfield. A touch of the rack, a length of rope and then a nice keen fire to roast the rascal. Go, Chamberlain, fetch your pen and write.' Then to another courtier, 'See these good fellows fed and bedded down.' So Little John and Much were taken into the buttery where they sat and ate their fill, then away to a corner of the servants' quarters to sleep soundly on rough mattresses by the light of tallow candles stuck in iron brackets on the wall.

Meanwhile, in Nottingham, the Sheriff had ordered the castle blacksmith to make an iron cage and fasten it to an old farm cart. When it was finished Robin, still bruised and bleeding from the fight, and still chained hand and foot, was dragged from the dungeon and flung into it then driven round the city with a notice round his neck, 'This is Robin Hood, traitor, outlaw and thief. Look on him well before he dies.' And extra guards were set over the city gates in case Robin's men should break out of the forest and try to rescue him when he was brought out to be hanged. Now it seemed there was no hope. Surely he would be executed as soon as the monk returned with instructions from Prince John.

Back at Westminster, the Prince's scrivener had written a letter and sealed it with the Royal Seal and Little John and Much were called into the presence once again, this time into the Royal Bedroom, where Prince John was standing stark naked in a huge wooden tub having a bath, with servants running to-and-fro ladling out some of the water already in the tub and adding fresh. And William, his private bath-man, was pouring the water over the Prince's shoulders and trying to whip up a lather with a large piece of soap made of mutton-fat and soda and fine wood-ash, scented with lavender. The Prince had five or six baths a year which made him one of the cleanest princes in Europe and he paid William a half-penny a day for his wages, and two-pence extra every time he actually had a bath.

As Little John and Much entered the room, the Prince was screaming that the water was too hot and that if William did not cool it he would have him roasted alive over one of the kitchen fires. But at last he calmed down, and when he had finished his bath and William was drying him off, he turned to Little John and Much.

'I have writ my answer to your Sheriff,' he said. 'I have no wish to visit his fair city of Nottingham. Let this Robin Hood be hanged without delay.' Then, 'Chamberlain,' he shrieked. 'Give these fellows the letter we wrote last night. And give them for their pains ten nobles each. My friends, we thank you. We wish you a pleasant journey home, and we wish your Robin Hood a pleasant hanging. And pray tell your Sheriff you have seen what few men on earth have seen – a naked prince, who one day will be king. There's something to brag about, and to tell your children!'

Little John and Much rode back as fast as their horses would carry them. It was now nearly a week since they had left Sherwood and ridden to London with the Sheriff's letter. They knew that the Sheriff had promised to wait until the monk returned with orders either to hang Robin in Nottingham or to bring him to be hanged in London. But he could easily kill Robin, pretending he had caught him trying to escape, or the castle guards who had lost twelve of their comrades in the church could try to get their revenge as Robin lay helpless in the dungeon. So every moment was precious.

The Prince's letter bore the royal seal, which meant that the city gate would be opened to them as soon as they showed it. But there was still a problem to be solved. Little John had spent a whole year in the Sheriff's service, pretending to be Reynold Greenleaf. If he was to deliver Prince John's letter in person, he would have to disguise himself or the Sheriff would surely recognise him.

So, when at last they reached Sherwood, the two weary riders rode into the camp where Little John had his hair cut and his beard trimmed into a fashionable shape. He and Much then dressed themselves in some of the fine clothes which were kept in their disguising store. So, next morning when they rode out to Nottingham, you would never have known they were the same two people.

After they had ridden three or four miles they discovered that Tricket had been following them a little way behind. It seemed she knew they were going to her master and that she might be able to help them. So they decided to take her along.

As they passed under the castle walls they saw men rigging up a gallows and stopped to speak to them.

'When is the hanging?' they asked. 'And who is to be hanged?'

'Tomorrow at dawn,' was the reply. 'And the man to be hanged is the outlaw Robin Hood who has plagued Sherwood for so long, and who last week murdered twelve of our comrades in St Mary's Church. Tomorrow will see the end of him.'

'Work hard and make your gallows strong,' said Much. 'We have heard of this Robin Hood in London. He is an evil fellow and deserves his fate.'

They had got back just in time!

When the Sheriff asked what had become of the monk who set out from London with the letter, Little John replied. 'Your monk, my Lord Sheriff, said such godly prayers that Prince John has made him Abbot of Westminster. Therefore we bring the answer in his stead.'

The Sheriff was happy to hear that the monk had been so successful, and he treated John and Much with great respect, putting them to sleep in a fine chamber only a little way from his own, telling his servants to treat them well and give them all they required in the way of food and drink and comfortable beds. So they bade him and his wife goodnight and, with Tricket at their heels, retired to their chamber. But not to sleep!

Waiting till the torches had burned low and all was quiet in the great hall, they took their swords and daggers and crept out along the gallery and down the massive oak stairway, treading tip-toe so as to make no sound; then along the dark passage which led down to the dungeons.

At the end of the passage there flickered a single torch, with a sentry standing in its shadow, guarding the iron doorway through which they now had to pass in order to get below. If the sentry challenged them and it came to a fight, they could easily kill him, but the noise would awaken the whole castle, which was the very thing they must avoid.

Little John and Much looked at each other and Much tapped himself on the chest as if to say 'Leave this to me.' Drawing his dagger he stole silently forwards, keeping in the shadows. When he was four or five yards away he suddenly made a swift spring and plunged his dagger up to the hilt in the sentry's left side, pressing it upwards towards his heart. The fellow had no time to cry out. He was already dead before he realised what had happened to him, and Little John ran to catch his body so that it would make no sound as it hit the floor.

Moving the dead man aside, Much knelt down and unhooked the keys from his belt while John took down the spluttering torch. Now they unlocked the iron door and started down the damp stairway leading below, with Tricket padding at their heels. Down, down they went, treading as silently as cats, until at last they heard voices and turning a corner saw a group of guards seated beside a brazier, drinking from a leather flagon and throwing dice upon the floor. These were the men who were to hang Robin in the morning and they were gambling to decide which one should have the pleasure of tying the rope around his neck and cracking the whip for the horse to pull the cart away. And they were laughing at the prospect.

They were big strong fellows but they were already half-drunk and three of them had unfastened their swords and piled them against the wall, never suspecting they were going to need

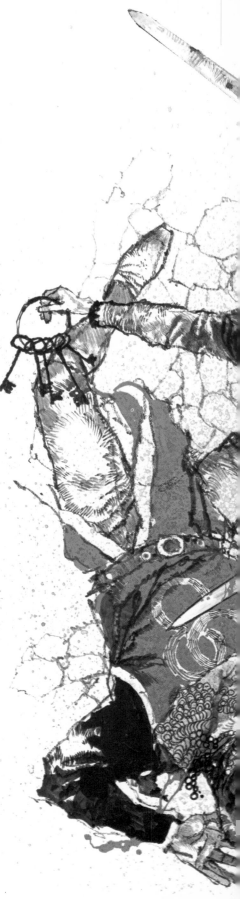

them. All the same it would be four against two, and Much was too small to be of any great help. The only way was to take them by some trick, and it was Much who thought of it.

Pulling John's head down beside his own he whispered softly, 'Follow me,' then took the lighted torch and uttering a wild scream rushed forward and hurled it into the middle of the game.

Suddenly all was panic. The guards stumbled to their feet but before they could recover from their surprise, Little John was amongst them, kicking the brazier over and lashing right and left with his sword. In a moment three of the guards lay dead and the fourth ran bleeding down the alleyway, pouring with blood from a wound in his head. Then all the prisoners in the dungeon, certain that someone had come to rescue them, began rattling their chains and beating on their bars while smoke poured from the overturned brazier and live coals were scattered all over the floor. It was like hell let loose.

Now John and Much had to be quick. This terrible noise would surely be heard in the castle above and spare guards would come rushing down to see what was amiss. 'Robin, Robin!' shouted John as they moved from cage to cage peering into the dark hollows to find the dear comrade and leader they had come to rescue. 'Where is Robin Hood?'

It was Tricket who found him. Suddenly she began barking and whining and clawing at the bars of one of the cages. And when Little John and Much came to her, there lay Robin chained to the wall, but wide awake and already tearing at his chains to try and free himself. In a few moments the door of his cage was open, the fetters on his feet unlocked and the chains loosened that bound him to the wall. At first he was so weak that he could hardly stand, but his fierce and eager spirit soon took control of his body as Tricket yapped and whined and leapt up to lick his face. Little John and Much clasped his hands and kissed him amid the smoke from the upturned brazier and the yelling of prisoners beating on iron and the fierce rattling of their chains.

'Now we must make all speed,' said Little John. 'Go, Much, unlock the doors. Set all the prisoners free. Give them the swords and daggers of the men we killed, or bars of iron, or chains to swing or blocks of stone to use as weapons. The castle guard may well be out by now. We cannot be too many or too strong.'

Then, as Much moved from cell to cell, unlocking the iron gates and setting the prisoners free, Little John shouted for silence and suddenly all was quiet. Pale and hungry men, dressed in filthy rags, some of whom had been in these foul dungeons for years, stole out and formed a ring round John and Much and Robin, the light of freedom burning in their eyes.

Then as Much handed out the weapons, Little John stepped forward and spoke. 'Comrades,' he said. 'We are still in deadly danger. We may have to cut our way through the castle guard before we reach the city gates and get to safety. Until we know if those above have heard us we must move like ghosts. If we reach the gates unseen and undetected, all will be easy. I mean to lead you to the forest where none can reach us. But we are not yet there. If I ask whether you would rather die free men than live chained up in darkness, what would your answer be?'

The answer came in a fierce whisper from twenty throats, 'To die free men rather than live as slaves,' and they crowded their half-starved bodies round Robin and Little John and Much and clutched forwards trying to lay their hands on them, as if by doing so they could share their strength and bravery.

'Then let us go,' said John, and the ghostly crew moved silently towards the stairs, padding along the stones with bare feet, the strong helping the weak, the young helping the aged.

At last they were in the great hall where the embers of the fire

still smouldered. They had not been heard, for the guards lay on the floor in drunken slumber. They had even forgotten to lock the huge oak doors which led into the open, so the ragged company passed silently into a night full of stars, only Tricket giving an occasional soft whine of pleasure as she trotted along besides Robin.

As they passed along Castle Rock, pressing themselves hard against the overhanging stone, a sentry guarding the ramparts above challenged them, but they froze and waited till he moved on, convinced that his ears had deceived him. There was now only one obstacle, the city gate, and this they could not avoid. If the guards were not asleep it would mean a fight.

Silently they moved on until there it was, guarded by six stout fellows fully armed and wide-awake.

John gathered the prisoners round him in the shadows.

'There is only one way,' he whispered softly. 'I will move over to the right and pretend the attack is coming from there. Four or five of the guards will run towards me, leaving the gate unprotected. While I am fighting them off you must get Robin and yourselves away to the greenwood.'

'But we cannot let you fight alone,' whispered Much. 'Take three or four of these stout fellows.' Then to the prisoners, 'Who is willing to die for Robin Hood?' At once a dozen half-starved hands were raised and voices whispered 'Me, take me, take me!'

In the ordinary way Robin would never have considered such a thing. It was his pride always to be in the front of the fight, always to be first to face any danger. But now, lean and hungry, with his wounds only half-healed he was happy for John to take command.

Little John chose three stout fellows from amongst the prisoners, giving them the swords and daggers and maces taken from the men they had killed in the dungeons below.

'When I cry out,' he said to Much, 'you must rush the gates and race for the forest. Robin's life is more precious than mine. His is the life of Liberty.'

John and the small group he had chosen moved silently to a point some distance away. Then suddenly John roared, 'A rescue! A rescue! Some help here. Ho! Come quick or Robin Hood, that mighty thief and traitor, will escape and the Lord High Sheriff will be put to shame. And many a guard will hang for failing in his watch and ward.'

At once four of the six guards ran towards the shouting while Much and the others rushed the main gate. They were only half armed, but they were sixteen against two and the two were soon overwhelmed. Within a few seconds they lay dead beside the guard house, and the prisoners were lifting the huge oaken bars from their sockets and swinging the gates wide open.

At first Robin wanted to go back to Little John. But Little John needed no helping hand. Already three of the guards who had rushed towards him when he cried for help were either dead or dying and the fourth was on his knees begging for mercy. John and his three ragged comrades left the fellow kneeling and were through the gate and away even before the bell began to toll its warning that the castle was being attacked.

That night there was great rejoicing in the camp. Robin was home again, a little tired but safe and well, and deep in the shelter of the cave Alice cleaned his wounds and anointed them with honey and bound them with clean bandages. And the outlaws made a mighty feast to welcome him back. And, along with the monk's servant who had been kept under guard all this time, eighteen prisoners took the greenwood oath.

At last, when the camp fire had burned low and only Little

John and Friar Tuck and Much and Will Scarlet were left sitting round Robin's rough couch, with Tricket lying quietly at his side, Robin took his crucifix and said a little prayer.

'I am alive and well and home again. Mother of God who watched over me, I thank you with all my heart and soul.' Then to Little John and Much, 'I thank you too.' Then patting Tricket's head, 'You too, dear and faithful friend.'

And Tricket licked his hand and brushed her tail to and fro across the floor, then nodded off to sleep.

CHAPTER TEN

Robin goes a-fishing

SOME books make out that Robin and his men won every battle and that it was only the Sheriff's men who got killed. But this is not true. Peter Colle, Jack Noakes, Will Browter, Amos Curdin, Matthew Wild and many others all died in one way or another, either shot by arrows or hacked down with swords or hanged. Their names were cut by Friar Tuck on one of the flat walls of the cave, and scratched above them were the words:

'These died that we might live. Requiescant in Pace,' which means 'We hope they rest happily when they come to Paradise.'

Then came the list, nearly thirty names in all, including Much the miller's son, who was caught by the Sheriff's men when he went secretly into Nottingham to buy flax for new bow strings. He was recognised by his slight limp, also by the scar down his left cheek which he got when he and Little John rescued Robin from the castle dungeon.

At first he told the Sheriff's men they were mistaken. He was no outlaw but an honest God-fearing citizen. But when they tortured him with thumb-screws and hung him from a beam with a kind of meat-hook, he gave in, admitting that he was indeed one of Robin's men. So they took him out and hanged him in the Market Square. He died bravely, refusing to betray any of the secret ways into the forest or the whereabouts of Robin's hiding places. He was ready to die rather than give Robin away.

When they heard what had happened John Silke, Simon Scales, and Peter Hoker stole into Nottingham at night and made their way to the pit where Much's body had been thrown and brought it back into the forest, Simon carrying it over his shoulders while John and Peter walked in front with drawn swords in case they should be attacked.

Meanwhile Robin had ordered a grave to be dug in the forest, and there he and Little John and the rest gathered in the moonlight, waiting to receive the dear brave body and lay it in the earth.

At last the sorrowful little party arrived and laid their burden down. And Robin himself helped to strip and bathe it in the stream and cross the hands upon its breast and wrap it in a white woollen shroud. Then they bound it to an oaken plank, with bow and quiver fastened along its side and lowered it into the grave. Friar Tuck spoke to Jesus and the Virgin Mary as it went down, asking them to take care of Much's soul and bring it safely into Heaven and let him be as brave and helpful there as he had been on earth. And Robin shed tears when he remembered the adventures that he and Much had passed through, the many dangers they had shared since that night in the crypt at Lastingham where they first met.

Whenever one of the outlaws died or was killed, Robin managed to get the news to the victim's mother and father or to his wife and family, sending messages secretly into villages and farms. Now he must do the same for Much. But Much was no local lad, born within reach of Sherwood or Barnsdale, he came from the far North, even further away than Hartoft. So Robin himself set out to carry the sad news.

On his way he made one of his secret visits to Hartoft, stealing into the farmhouse at dead of night, waking Mark and Marian in the still small hours and sitting whispering in their tiny bedrooms, telling them all his news and hearing theirs. Then he slipped away, through Lealholm and Stonegate, on to Mickleby.

Much's father had died of the burns he received when their home was fired, but his mother was still alive and well. She wept when she heard that Much was dead, but was proud when Robin told her what a fine comrade he had been and how bravely he had died and what a beautiful funeral they had given him. So they knelt together and said a little prayer for Much's soul asking Jesus to make him happy in Paradise and give him some useful work to do, not just playing a harp and singing.

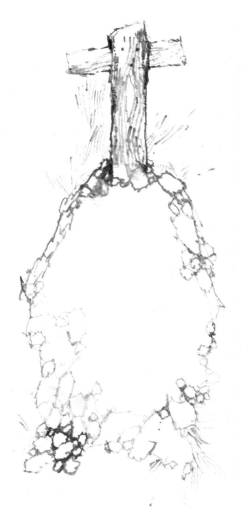

*   *   *   *

Now it was while he was in the north that Robin had a strange adventure, this time not in the greenwood but on the open sea. He was standing beside the tiny bay at Runswick one morning, watching some fishermen prepare their boat for sea and wondering what it must be like to live that kind of life, tossed about by the waves and every day feeling the salt spray in your mouth, when the chief fisherman spoke to him:

'Good morrow, lad. I see by your garb and by your bow and quiver that you are a landlubber. How would you like to learn how fishermen live?'

'I would indeed if you have room for me,' said Robin.

'Oh, we can fit him in can't we? He can count the fish!'

So Robin jumped aboard and the boat pushed off. He laid his bow and quiver aside and for a while sat beside the steersman enjoying the breeze and the hiss of the spray as it shot past the boat's bows, and watching the men working the ropes and getting ready their nets.

But soon he began to feel sick and wished he had not been so quick to accept the fishermen's invitation to crew-up with them. For their part they laughed and poked a little quiet fun at him.

'Now perhaps you will learn to appreciate the fish you eat,' said the Captain, as they heaved in a net-full of gleaming silver herring and poured them down the hatch at Robin's feet. And once again the rest of the crew laughed.

But the last laugh was to be with Robin. For suddenly another boat hove in sight, two or three times as big as their own; and a fellow standing at her forepeak challenged them and told them to heave to. 'We are a pirate ship,' he said, 'seeking a catch of herring without having to work for it. We have already boarded two boats and when their crews resisted, have heaved them overboard and let them drown.' He pointed to a half-naked body swinging upside down from the yardarm. 'That fellow was one of their skippers,' he said. 'We fished him out and chopped him up on the deck. The same will happen to you if you do not give up your catch.'

'Better to lose our catch,' said Robin's Captain, 'than lose our lives. I see no help for it, we must give in. They are three times as big as us.'

'No help?' said Robin, his sickness suddenly leaving him. 'Give me my bow.'

In a flash he was balancing on one of the thwarts, laying an arrow on the bowstring. Then he took aim at the fellow on the forepeak of the pirate ship and let fly. The arrow caught the pirate in the throat, went right through his neck and was standing out eight or ten inches behind it. He gave a strangled scream, pitched headlong into the sea and disappeared.

'Now lash me to the mast,' said Robin. 'This heaving deck is no place for an archer to plant his feet. And pass me my quiver.' He stood with arms outspread while one of the crew took a couple of turns round his waist, tying him with a bowline securely to the mast. Now he was ready.

Soon another of the pirate crew appeared wondering what had happened to his mate. He was a great brawny red-headed fellow with two teeth missing in the front. He looked around him, then roared down to Robin, 'Hey, what's happened to my mate?'

'This,' said Robin, and a second arrow winged its way upwards catching the brawny fellow full in the chest. He did not fall overboard but sprawled on the deck, writhing and kicking and screaming for a few moments before he died.

Then the rest of the pirates began to appear, asking each other why the little boat had not yet surrendered. And one by one they were shot dead by the slim fellow in the well-worn suit of green, with red-brown hood, lashed to the mast of the tiny fishing boat. Some plunged overboard, others fell spinning down their own hatches, clutching at the arrow shafts and trying to pull them out before they died. Eleven of the crew were served in this way and it seemed that that was the end of the matter. But then the pirate Captain appeared, a great black-bearded fellow in a woollen cap. He looked around astonished, hardly able to believe his eyes. Around him lay his crew, all pierced by arrows and either dead or dying and his own end not far away.

'That is how we deal with pirates,' shouted Robin. 'And here's a taste for you.'

The last arrow flew and caught the pirate skipper under the heart. He clutched at the shaft, roaring with pain and trying to drag it out. But he was not yet dead. He must be finished off. As he spun round, looking down in astonishment at the tiny boat that was attacking him, a second arrow caught him behind the ear and entered his brain and he too fell among his evil comrades. The job was finished.

Now Robin was untied from the mast and two of the crew swarmed up the side of the pirate ship and heaved the dead bodies overboard, then swabbed the decks clean. Then from the forepeak cast a tow line across to their own boat and made it fast.

The pirate ship was heavy and hard to work and it was a long way back to Runswick. Indeed, it was more than a week before they did get back, for a storm came up and a full north-easter blew. So they were forced from their course and finally driven ashore at a tiny harbour further south, which ever since then has been called Robin Hood's Bay, in memory of the time, the only time in his life, that Robin became a fisherman.

CHAPTER ELEVEN

Robin meets his Match!

IT was now three years since Robin had become an outlaw. Mark and Marian were seventeen, both of them strong and handsome and overflowing with energy and high spirits. Every day since Robin left they had practised with bow and arrow, quarterstaff and broadsword, so that if ever Robin returned they could show him how hard they had worked and how much they owed to his teaching. And always Marian was the best, especially with the broadsword which she loved. She had wrists of steel, was like a cat on her feet and was absolutely fearless. It was as if she had been born to it.

Now Hartoft, along with the forest and farmlands around it, belonged to Sir Guy of Gisburn, a young man of fierce and ugly temper whose grandfather had saved the life of its former owner, the Lord of Pickering, in the Battle of the Standard back in 1138 and had been given Hartoft as a reward.

Sir Guy's real home was the village from which his family took its name, Gisburn, in the West Riding of Yorkshire not far from Settle. He only made the long journey across to the North Yorkshire Moors when he wanted to make sure that his forest was being well looked after and his fields properly tilled. And when he did come, he came alone or with very few attendants.

It was on one of these rare visits that Mark and Marian's father took it into his head to send a message saying that they would be honoured if Sir Guy would sup with them one evening and share a bowl of wine. After all, he was the Lord of their land (or landlord as we say today) and it was therefore their duty to show him proper courtesy and respect. Sir Guy replied that he would be happy to join them and he named both the day and the hour.

Sir Guy was thirty years old, a widower full of angry energy. It was now two years since his wife and baby had died and he was eager to marry again. When he saw Marian his eyes lit up and he began to think what a fine wife she would make and what a dashing figure she would cut in Gisburn Hall.

So after dinner, when Mark and Marian had retired to their rooms and the two men were alone together, he told Marian's father that he would like to marry her and that he hoped she would learn to love him and would give him the children he sorely longed for. He said he was a kindly man and was sure he could make Marian happy. She could ride across to Hartoft every month or so and her father and Mark would always be welcome to visit her in Gisburn. He said he was leaving in two days' time and would like to take her back with him to prepare for the wedding.

Marian's father could not help feeling how wonderful it would be for his daughter to marry a nobleman and how much he would enjoy seeing the people of Hartoft bow and curtsey to her, calling her 'My Lady'. In any case Sir Guy could easily turn them out of the farm if they offended him. So it did not take him long to make up his mind.

'If the girl is willing you may count her yours,' he said. And he sent a servant to bring Marian down from her room.

When Marian learned that Sir Guy wanted to marry her she bowed her head and blushed, pretending that she was honoured, but begging for a few days grace to prepare herself for the journey. 'Grant me a week,' she said, as she went down on her knees and kissed Sir Guy's hand in token of agreement. 'Then my father himself will bring me to you.' At this Sir Guy laughed and pulled her to her feet.

'Your wish is granted,' he said. 'I will go back and make all ready. A week from now the wedding bells shall ring.' Then he let go of her and she fled back to her room trying to hide her anger and distress.

What was she to do? She and Mark loved their father and always tried to follow his wishes. But she could never marry a man she did not love, a man she hardly knew. And then, as she sat on her bed trying to calm herself and clear her mind, it suddenly came over her like a flash of lightning that there was someone she did know, someone she did love: and that he was the only one she ever could love. His name was Robin Hood.

Her father would be hurt, Sir Guy would be angry and might even try to take revenge, but it was useless to resist. Her heart thundered its message loud and clear and although she only whispered them, the words seemed to fill the whole sky. 'I belong to Robin and to him alone. I must go and seek him out. I must! I must!'

So late that night when Sir Guy had gone and the whole house was asleep, she crept into Mark's room and woke him, telling him what had happened.

'I could never see it through,' she said, 'to wed a man I do not love. Besides, my heart is promised to another.'

'To Robin?' said Mark.

'Yes,' replied Marian. 'To him alone. I meant to wait a while but now it seems the die is cast. I shall leave tonight. There is no time to lose.'

'You cannot go alone,' said Mark. 'The way is dangerous. I must come with you.'

'No, you must stay,' said Marian. 'When by the week's end I have not come to Gisburn, Sir Guy will come to fetch me. Our father will tell him I have run away. Sir Guy will not believe him. You can confirm that what he says is true and that neither he nor you were party to it.' Then she added, 'I mean to go disguised. You and I are of a size. You have spare stockings, buckskin boots and jerkin. They will fit me like a glove. I know the way, eastwards to Pickering, then turning south. I shall hide by day and travel by night. Believe me I shall take no harm.'

At this, she began to undress and Mark took his rough forest clothes out of the cupboard and helped her into them. Then he took her hair and coiled it into a thick rope and fastened it under her cap with a bronze pin, fitting the cap firmly over the coil. Next he put a hood over her shoulders and laced it up the front, then gave her his broadsword and dagger and helped her buckle them on. Lastly he threw his winter cloak around her and stood back to see the effect.

'Perfect,' he said. 'You pass the test. Keep to the woodland tracks and if you must speak, speak in manly tones, low down.'

As they crept downstairs the sleeping housedogs stirred and growled just as they had when Robin left three years ago. But when Marian bent down and patted them they licked her hand and nodded off to sleep again.

Very quietly Mark lifted the door latch and they stepped out into the moonlight.

'I will come with you to the gate,' said Mark, and away they went, treading silently in their soft buckskin boots, and soon reached the opening in the fence which closed off the farmyard from its fields and from the open forest.

'You are right to leave,' whispered Mark. 'But life will be very empty here without you.'

He clasped her in his arms and held her close and kissed her. For seventeen years they had scarcely spent a single day apart. They had been half each other's lives, a single mind inside two bodies. Now she was being torn away from him, perhaps forever. He looked into her eyes and tried to hide his misery with a laugh. Then suddenly she was gone. He watched her down the long pathway, saw her turn and wave a last goodbye as she plunged into the forest. Then he went back into the house, climbed the stairway, lay down on his bed and burst into tears.

*   *   *   *

Now Marian had only one thought in her mind – to put as many miles as possible between herself and Helmsley, where Sir Guy was quartered. So once in the forest she struck eastwards, through Cropton, then south to Cawthorn Moor. Skirting the Roman camp she slanted left past Saintoft Grange and on towards Pickering.

But suddenly she was frightened. It was one thing to dress as a boy and cut one's hair and wear a belt and broadsword, but what if she failed to carry it off? What if people saw that it was all a pretence? She tried speaking low-down and manly as Mark had told her to. She lengthened her stride and planted her feet more firmly on the ground and gazed around her bravely and put on a bold swagger. Then she started whistling to keep her courage up. And so marched into Pickering.

By this time it was six o'clock and the village was already astir. Labourers were on their way to work, men-at-arms in chainmail stood guarding the entrance to the castle, somewhere a blacksmith was beating on his anvil, a bell was calling people to morning Mass and women were fetching water from the stream.

Marian sat down beside the village green to take a bite of bread and cheese, but scarcely had she opened her pack when a cart loaded with barrels came rumbling along the path from

Kingthorpe way, past Manor Farm and Shepherd Hill, driven by a kindly-looking, weatherbeaten man of middle age.

''Tis now or never,' thought Marian. 'He travels south and so do I. Perhaps we could journey together.' Then, as the cart was almost on top of her, she plucked up all her courage and shouted bold and friendly:

'Good morrow, Carter. May I beg a lift?' The carter pulled up and wiped his brow.

'Where are you bound for, lad?' he asked.

('That was a good start, calling me lad,' thought Marian.)

'I travel south,' she said, gaining confidence with every word she spoke. 'To London. My brother is a soldier there. He helps to guard the Tower. I go to join him. 'Tis a good life.'

'Get up beside me,' said the carter, as he moved aside to make room on his narrow seat.

'You must have started early with your load,' said Marian as they started off.

'From Goatland before dawn, and down through Saltergate.'

'Do you travel far?'

'To York,' said the carter. 'To sell my load. Eight hundred pounds of salt from Saintoft and from Guisborough. The monks there work the pans. 'Tis a great skill. No-one knows quite how old. But Guisborough salt is famous. It fetches a good price at market.'

'I have never seen a proper market,' said Marian. 'Only the tiny one they hold in Kirkbymoorside. This is the furthest I have ever been from home. In our village nothing happens from year's end to year's end. 'Tis slow and lazy. Besides, the girls there are all plain. In London I may find a comely wife.'

The carter laughed. 'You are too young to marry,' he said.

'I am long past twenty,' lied Marian.

'What is your name?'

''Tis Mark. Mark Walbere. What is yours?'

'My name is Peter Heckle,' said the carter. 'I make this journey twice a year, in autumn.'

So they travelled on together, enjoying each other's company. And the carter told Marian how the monks at Guisborough took salt water from the springs in the Abbey grounds and heated it in huge copper vats until only the salt was left and how in the end they had enough salt not only for themselves, but some to sell. For in those far-off days when winter feed was hard to come by, most of the cattle, sheep and pigs were killed in October or November and salted down to last till spring. Salt was one of the most useful things you could buy and salters were some of the most important people in the land.

They passed on through Malton towards York and soon saw

the Minster towering above the rest of the city. Passing through Monkgate into Goodramgate, they found themselves in the Shambles, with Newgate and Swinegate and Peasgate on their right. Here Marian saw things that she had never seen before; stalls set up in the street and goods for sale, a busy market place. In Coney Street good woollen cloth from Ripon and from Knaresborough, in Patrick Pool and Jubergate fine linen, on Peasholm Green all sorts of leather goods, in Colliergate pewter and pottery, in Walmgate gloves and barrels, hats and hemp, in Fossgate pots and pans and in an alley leading off it, sugar and lemons and figs and apricots and plums and melons and dates and a fine new cloth called damask, all brought from the East and very rare. In Market Street fish and bread and meat and the whole point of Peter's journey, salt.

So it was at Matthew Salter's house that they stopped to unload their barrels. And Matthew asked them in and offered them each a mug of ale and gave Peter a good price for his salt. Then Peter and Marian went out to fill the cart with cloth and leather goods and hemp and pewter-ware, things that the monks at Guisborough needed, things they could neither make nor buy at home.

Soon came the time for parting, Peter to return to Malton and the north, Marian to journey southwards through Eskrick, Riccall, Barlby, Selby, Snaith and Finningly.

At last, after six days of walking she found herself on the northern edge of Sherwood. Now she knew that Robin could not be very far away, and now I am going to tell you how she found him.

Robin often went for long walks in the forest, all by himself. He loved his outlaw army and enjoyed all the business of the camp, but he had to be ever on the alert, watching and listening, visiting look-out posts and hiding places, sometimes slipping into Nottingham to learn the latest news; and this he could best do on his own.

The day after Marian came to the forest he was out on one of these patrols when he suddenly heard twigs being broken underfoot a little way ahead. He stepped aside from the path and waited, listening. Soon, from his hiding place, he saw a young man approaching down the glade. He was tall and strong and carried only a dagger and broadsword. For a moment it crossed Robin's mind that he had seen this young fellow before, but he dismissed the thought as he stepped out to challenge him.

'What is your business here in the forest?' he asked.

Marian's heart gave a great leap as she recognised him, standing there so slim and brave and handsome and she longed to rush into his arms and cover him with kisses. But then she had another thought. There would be time for kisses later on. She had travelled ninety-odd miles pretending to be a man and

no-one had found her out. Why give herself away so soon? So she stood her ground.

'What is my business here, you ask. I ask you what is yours?'

'You are now in outlaw country,' said Robin. 'We do not suffer strangers in the greenwood. You were best go back the way you came.'

'No outlaw shall make me go back,' said Marian, and she drew her sword. 'Come, let us fight it out and may the best man win.'

She stood there so fierce and challenging and her voice rang out so manly that Robin had no alternative but to draw his sword and face the matter out. And so the fight began.

Robin was a fine swordsman but Marian surprised him with her skill and toughness. She could catch him off-balance and make him miss his stroke, and when he made a dangerous cut could turn his blade aside with hers. Best trick of all, she twice changed hands and fought him left-to-right as boxers sometimes do. They call them Southpaws. But at last Robin began to wear her down. Now he must surely win. But then she saw her chance. Behind him was a chestnut tree with a root sticking out of the ground in a sort of loop. Most swordsmen were careful to see that all was clear behind them. But this time Robin had forgotten.

With a last great effort Marian attacked and drove him backwards into the trap. His foot caught in the root, his sword flew out of his hand and down he went, head over heels in the bracken. In a moment Marian's sword was at his throat. Robin tried to reach for his horn but she planted her foot on it and held it fast, then slashed its cord and bending down, picked up the horn herself.

'Now fellow,' she said. 'Get up and tramp! I want to see your outlaw band and the place they bide in. I also want to meet their leader and tell him how I met you sword to sword and beat you to your knees.'

There was no way Robin could get out of it. He had to obey. Scrambling to his feet he stood there helpless, and feeling rather foolish.

'Now put your hands up, about face and march,' said Marian. 'Try any tricks with me and you will get this blade between your shoulders.'

'What of my sword?' said Robin.

'I will take care of that,' said Marian, picking it up.

It was comical to see Robin returning to camp as a prisoner. But what followed was more comical still. As the outlaws clustered round, Marian spoke out in a ringing voice.

'Fetch me your leader. I come to marry him.'

At this the outlaws laughed. 'Our leader is no woman, but the man who stands at your sword's point.'

'This fellow lead?' said Marian. 'Why he cannot even hold his own against a woman.'

Then she let out a peal of laughter and dropped her sword. 'I am no man as I appear, but Robin's pupil Marian. Three years ago I vowed to wed him when the time was ripe,' and with that she snatched off her cap and her hair fell tumbling over her shoulders and she rushed into Robin's arms hugging him, and laughing and crying by turns, and Tricket was rushing round yelping like a mad thing as she recognised the voice that had shouted 'Stop!' in the Forest Court three years before.

A few days later Robin and Marian became husband and wife. The outlaws were all for a greenwood wedding, performed by Friar Tuck. But Robin insisted they be wed in church. So in the end they had two weddings, first in the forest, kneeling side by side in the tiny chapel amongst the trees, then in the little Norman church at Edwinstone, where you can still see the ancient door through which they passed to reach the altar, while Will Scarlet and twenty archers kept guard amongst the trees outside in case of ambush.

Little John gave Marian away and Alice was her bridesmaid and Alan a'Dale was Robin's best man. And after the wedding they carried the old priest away with them into the greenwood and gave him twenty golden nobles for his pains and toasted him in Gascon wine and as he was not used to drinking he got rather tiddly and had to stay the night.

So Marian came to the greenwood, and the outlaws never wearied of hearing how she fought the Prince of Outlaws sword to sword and how she made him yield.

*   *   *   *

Now in the bustle and excitement of the wedding, they forgot that Sir Guy was expecting Marian's father to bring her across to Gisburn within the next few days and that he would be very angry when she did not arrive and that he would probably come back to Hartoft to fetch her. It was now ten days since Marian had escaped and Mark and her father might already be in great danger. So it was agreed that Little John should get together a raiding party, eighteen or twenty strong, to move swiftly north and bring Mark and his father down to Sherwood, along with a few of their faithful servants.

Little John began choosing his men, including Will Sawyer, Mark Tardiffe, Jacob Hobbe and John Miles with his young brother Jack who was the best at finding his way across country in the dark.

But they were too late. Sir Guy had already returned to

Hartoft and finding Marian missing had taken his revenge. It was Mark himself who brought the news. He staggered into camp one morning pale and footsore. He had travelled the ninety-odd miles from the north with little food and scarcely any sleep and the news he brought was even worse than they had feared. Sir Guy had waited only a few days before returning with half-a-dozen of his servants, ready for mischief. Finding Marian gone he had shouted insults at her father, then in a rage had started smashing up the farm, in the end setting fire to it and burning it to the ground, killing the housedogs and leaving the place a ruin. Their father had taken his broadsword and tried to defend himself but had been cut down by Sir Guy and his body left among the blazing ruins.

Mark was out in the forest at the time and had been warned by one of the villagers that he would be killed if he showed himself. Waiting 'till night-fall he had lifted his father's body from the heap of charred timbers and buried it in the orchard behind the farmhouse, then started for Sherwood with all speed.

CHAPTER TWELVE

Sir Guy of Gisburn

WHEN Robin heard what had happened at Hartoft he turned pale, holding Marian very close to comfort her, murmuring how dearly he loved her. Then, telling Will Scarlet to take Mark into the warm and see him fed, he called Little John and Friar Tuck aside and whispered to them, 'As soon as it is dark, I shall make my way North.'

'To Hartoft?' said Little John.

'To Gisburn,' said Robin. 'I have a debt to pay.'

'Let us come with you,' said the Friar.

'No,' said Robin. 'This is a private quarrel.'

'There will be danger. He will be guarded.'

'This life is full of dangers,' replied Robin.

'Take one of us.'

'I think it better to hunt alone. You are my second-in-command and you my third. If worst comes to worst, if I am not back within the month, you must take charge. You know all that I know, the places, tracks, the roads, the rules. I shall not be missed.'

Seeing that he was set on going, Little John and Friar Tuck said no more. They knew they could not change his mind, and knowing what had happened back at Hartoft, they had no wish to change it.

So Robin armed himself and wrapped his cloak around him and slipped away into the forest without even saying goodbye to Marian. The truth was he could not trust himself. She knew him so well, she would guess what he had in mind and would try to persuade him not to go. It was better to leave quickly, without more words.

He knew that Gisburn lay to the north-west, not far from Barnoldswick and Settle. For four days he travelled hard, sometimes along the tracks used by shepherds or drovers, sometimes through thick forest, sometimes high up across the open moor.

At last he reached a wide stretch of ploughland carved from the forest itself, and a ploughman resting his team of oxen at the end of a furrow.

'How far to Gisburn, friend?'

'The forest here is Trawden. Yonder is Pendle. Follow the path until you reach the stream. Follow the stream down through the gill. There will be Gisburn, on your left. A ten mile tramp.'

'Who is your Lord?'

'Sir Guy.'

'Of Gisburn?'

'Yea. And would he were not.'

'You do not like him then?'

'He is ill-liked by all. He has an evil heart, a vicious temper and a violent hand. Murdered his wife and infant son. Left them to starve and rot, chained each to other in the cave beneath his home because he claimed the child was none of his. He has slain many hereabouts and taken many maids against their will. None dares oppose him, for he is strong and brave and skilled in arms. What would you with him?'

'He has done foul wrong to one I dearly love. I come to punish him.'

'Young man, you face a cruel task. Many have tried to bring him low but all have failed. 'Tis said the Devil guards him.'

'How shall I meet him, face to face, unguarded?'

'He hunts the stag. Alone. He knows the forest as I know these fields. We live in fear of him. We sleep with doors close-barred. We watch our women.'

'Alone, you say?'

'Alone.'

''Tis well.'

'He is skilled in weapons, rides hard, fights fiercely with the sword, and what is rare in men of rank, uses the bow. He challenges the common archers, often splits the wand and bears away the prize.'

Now Robin knew he had only to wait. For days he wandered the forest, watching, listening. Sometimes he lay in broken cattle sheds, sometimes sheltered under overhanging rocks, begging his bread from friendly woodmen, shepherds or hurdlemakers, labourers in field and forest. Waiting, watching.

Then one morning it happened. He was standing on the edge of a long glade amongst a clump of ash and sweet chestnut. The sun was not yet fully risen and the trees seemed to spring from the low mist instead of from the forest floor. Suddenly he heard the sound of branches being moved aside, and footfalls. Into the glade walked a tall black-bearded figure with powerful shoulders, wearing a broadsword and bearing bow and quiver.

Robin stepped from hiding into the open and the two stood

facing one another some twenty yards apart. Robin was the first to speak.

'You are the Lord of Gisburn?'

'I am. The land you trespass on is mine.'

'Forget the trespass. That can wait. I come to pay a debt. For what you did at Hartoft some weeks since. To one I love and to his hearth and home.'

Then, after a moment's silence, very quietly. 'My name is Robin Hood.'

Without another word they dropped their bows and loosed their quivers, then drew their swords and flew at each other, slashing with all their force. Steel clashed on steel, the forest rang and birds flew screaming from the trees. Backwards and forwards swayed the fight. First Robin had the advantage, pressing Sir Guy back to the edge of the glade. Then Robin's sword struck a branch which made him lose his balance and fall to one knee. In a flash, Sir Guy rushed at him aiming a deadly thrust at his head. Luckily Robin managed to parry it and scramble to his feet. But Sir Guy pressed forward and it seemed that he must surely win. He was so strong, so fierce, so skilful. The battle swayed backwards and forwards close on half-an-hour, until both fighters were exhausted, breaking away from each other at the very same moment, to rest and get their breath.

'It seems,' said Robin, 'that we are equally matched. We could be fighting here till sundown.'

Then never daring to think that Sir Guy would accept, 'Why not try me bow to bow?'

In spite of his cruelty and evil ways, Sir Guy of Gisburn was no coward. Besides, he had so often triumphed at the butts that he believed few men could beat him. So he accepted Robin's challenge. Never taking their eyes from each other the two men moved to where they had first thrown down their bows. Each drew an arrow from its quiver and stood stock-still waiting for the other to stir.

Sir Guy was standing slightly in the shadows, with his back to a huge oak tree, while Robin stood in the open, clear to be seen. Suddenly, with cat-like speed, Sir Guy snatched his arrow and took aim, pressing the bow forwards towards the arrow's head. But he was too late. He had met the greatest archer in England, the greatest in the world. Before his bow was fully bent, Robin's arrow was on its way. The aim was sure, it carried his last ounce of strength. It caught Sir Guy beneath the heart and went right through him, nailing him to the tree. The bow and arrow fell from his hands and there he hung, stark dead, his eyes still open and his jaw slightly dropped as if he were about to speak. Robin had paid his debt.

CHAPTER THIRTEEN

The Silver Arrow

THE Sheriff had been very angry when Little John and Much helped Robin to escape from prison. He had looked forward to seeing his enemy dragged through the streets of Nottingham and hanged outside the city walls. Then the outlaws would have been without their great leader and it would have been much easier to catch them. Now he had to think of another plan.

He knew that Robin and his men were proud of being such great bowmen and that they could not resist entering every contest they possibly could. So he arranged a very special one, 'To choose the Finest Archer in the Land,' the winner to receive 'A Silver Arrow lying on Crimson Velvet in a Handsome Jewelled Box, emblazoned with the city's Coat of Arms. Also fifty nobles in a leather purse.' Surely that would tempt Robin Hood to come into the city!

Little John and Friar Tuck and Marian tried to persuade him not to take the risk. 'Remember what happened last time,' they said. But Robin wouldn't listen.

'My credit is at stake,' he said. 'My name and fame. I am the greatest archer in the land! For all our sakes I must defend my title.' Then he told them how he meant to do it. But made them swear to keep it a dead secret.

So they agreed to let him try his luck and arranged that twenty of his best men should mingle with the crowd while another hundred lay ready on the edge of the forest to help in case of need.

At last the great day came, with flags flying from the grandstand and crowds gathering to enjoy the fun and cheer their favourites on. From Lancashire they came and from Lincolnshire, from Yorkshire and Warwickshire, from Charnwood Forest and from Cannock Chase, from Market Deeping and from Lutterworth, from Thrapston, Turnditch, Dronfield, Congleton and Rockingham, as well as from villages near at home. One party had even made its way down from

Bowland and another from Rossendale and there were two from Knaresborough and one from Pateley Bridge. One hundred and sixty of the finest archers in the land, all eager to carry off the prize, each man to shoot a dozen arrows at the target eighty yards away.

There they stood loosening their shoulders, tying on their bracers, taking bowstrings from their linen bags and smoothing them with wax, stroking their bows and even whispering to them as riders often whisper to a horse.

At last in a blare of trumpets came the Sheriff and his wife, with friends and members of their household, followed by the castle guards, one hundred men in shirts of mail, their leather helmets strengthened with an iron rim and cross-piece, each man with a bow and quiver-full of arrows. Some stationed themselves close to the Sheriff and his party, some stood on the flanks of the pavilion, others stood round the shooting mark or near the target. The rest mingled with the crowd.

Meanwhile Robin's twenty were also there, standing lazily on the outskirts of the range, their bows and quivers close at hand. And hidden away on the edge of the forest another hundred waiting to spring out at the first blast of Robin's silver horn. But Robin himself was nowhere to be seen and no-one had any news of him.

As each party arrived, they gave the name of their champion to a scribe who wrote it down on parchment, and when it seemed that no more entries would arrive, the scribe handed the list to the herald whose task it was to announce the names of the competitors as they stepped up to the mark.

This was one of the greatest days in the whole history of the longbow. Archer after archer filled the target with his shafts all tightly packed close to the centre and the judges found it very hard to choose one from another. As the herald's voice rang out, giving each man's score, the crowds cheered and shook their champions by the hand or lifted them shoulder high. The trumpets sounded and the banners waved and the sun shone out in splendour.

At last the winner was announced. John Pyke from Needwood in the Vale of Trent. He and five others had hit the centre of the target nine times out of twelve, but in the shoot-off he had beaten them all with ten, all planted squarely in the clout, with two more close beside them. So the trumpet sounded and the herald's voice rang out across the range, 'The winner of the Silver Arrow and the finest archer in the land, John Pyke from Needwood in the Vale of Trent. Step forth John Pyke and take your well-earned prize.'

John Pyke stepped forward, or rather was carried forward on the shoulders of his supporters and the Sheriff took the jewelled case and opened it, showing the Silver Arrow to the crowd. But even as he did so, a voice rang out above the shouting and cheering. 'Tarry a moment! A late-comer who has travelled far would try his skill against John Pyke of Trent.' The crowd turned to where the challenge came from and there, his knees fastened with leather straps to a pair of oaken boards and his hands holding what looked like a pair of wooden clogs, was a cripple in ragged garments, with coal-black beard and a patch over his left eye; at his side a young lad carrying a bow and quiver.

'Never a moment more!' shouted the Sheriff. 'The game is done! John Pyke has swept the field!'

'Would John Pyke wish to take the Silver Arrow while a better archer had no chance to shoot?' shouted the cripple.

'Who is this archer and where is his home? Why comes he late to meet the challenge?' cried the Sheriff.

''Tis I. Tom Werkin of the Wold,' said the cripple. 'Before John Pyke receives the prize I challenge him to shoot with me, to learn if he be best man here or no.'

'You, a cripple,' said the Sheriff. 'How can you hold a bow?'

'I bent a bow for England overseas. Fighting in Normandy I won these wounds. But still my arm is strong, my aim is steady and my one eye clear.'

'Enough, enough!' shouted John Pyke. 'Come, let us shoot it out!' And all his fellows echoed him, 'Yea, let them shoot!'

So the crowd parted to make way for the cripple who came forward on all fours, followed by his boy. Now the crowd was hushed. How was it possible for a man so maimed to hold a bow and shoot? Surely he must be trying to make a fool of them. Yet his challenge had been so fierce and manly that they watched and wondered as he hobbled forwards.

They drew straws for the order of shooting and John Pyke drew the longest. So a new target was brought out and he took his place at the mark. Eleven shafts struck home dead centre and the other one was only a little wide. He had never shot so well, and, my goodness, how the crowd roared and shouted! 'Pyke for the Silver Arrow! Pyke is best!'

But now the cripple had laid aside his clogs and was flexing his shoulders. The judges cleared the arrows from the target. The cripple hobbled forward on his knees, then took his bow in hand. Holding it cross-ways instead of upright he now took aim. No-one had ever seen an archer shoot with a bow held crossways. Surely it had to be upright, with the string pulled up beside the archer's ear!

But this man had learned a new way of shooting. As fast as his boy handed him the arrows he took aim and shot, all twelve dead centre, the last one splitting three already fastened to the target. Suddenly the crowd went wild. All twelve arrows in the centre! They had never seen such shooting! It was not to be

believed! The cripple had won! Now the trumpets sounded
again and after much flurrying and consulting with the Sheriff,
the herald made a fresh announcement.

'The late entry, Tom Werkin of the Wold, has won the prize.'

And there were John Pyke and Tom Werkin shaking hands
in the midst of the milling crowd, congratulating each other.

'Come forward to receive your prize, Tom Werkin of the
Wold,' shouted the herald.

The cripple took up his clogs and began slowly to climb the
steps which led to the Sheriff's platform. Now came the test.
Sitting up there watching the contest the Sheriff had been
twenty yards away. Now they would be almost touching each
other. Still the cripple pressed forward until only a few feet
separated them. Then he laid down his clogs and looking the
Sheriff boldly in the face, stretched out his hand to receive the
prize. But the Sheriff, already suspicious, paused a moment, then
suddenly bent down and snatched the patch from the cripple's
eye.

'You are no cripple!' he roared. 'You are Robin Hood! Seize
on him fellows! Clap him in our dungeon!'

But even as he spoke, Robin (yes, the cripple was Robin in
disguise!) drew his hunting knife and slashed the leather straps
that held his legs, then took his horn from his jerkin and blew
three silvery blasts. In a moment all hell broke loose. Twenty
men seized their bows and quivers and the hundred hiding in
the greenwood came rushing on to the range, shooting arrows
like a hail as they advanced. In a moment the crowd had
scattered and it was a straight fight between the Sheriff's guard
and the outlaws. In the end thirty men lay dead, including five
of Robin's.

At last the outlaws had driven the Sheriff's guard right back
to the city gate and were eager to go on fighting until they had
well and truly beaten them. But Robin thought they had already
taught the Sheriff's men a good enough lesson. If they ventured

further they might be trapped. So he gave the order to break off the fight and return to the forest.

Carrying their five dead comrades and helping the wounded along as best they could, he and his men began to retreat. But the Sheriff's men suddenly rallied and began to follow them, shouting curses and firing arrows thick and fast. Most of the outlaws reached the shelter of the forest without much difficulty, but the rest had to fight their way backwards mile after mile across the countryside until at last they saw the castle of Sir Richard of the Lea only half a mile away. Still fighting hard they reached the outer wall and thundered at its gate. Sir Richard himself came out to let them in, twenty weary archers led by Little John and Will Scarlet.

When they were safe inside Sir Richard shut the gate and bolted it and his wife and her women took in the wounded, to bathe and bandage them. So ended the 'Shooting for the Silver Arrow' in which Robin proved himself to be the greatest archer in the land.

But now the castle was besieged. The Sheriff's men gathered around it and as evening fell others joined them, until there were three hundred throats all shouting insults to Sir Richard, calling him traitor to the king and miscreant knight.

At last the Sheriff himself arrived. Standing in the centre of the throng, he shouted to Sir Richard to come out and fight. 'Coward!' he called. 'You dare not face our steel. Give me the chance to meet you sword to sword.' But Sir Richard was not to be tempted to leave the shelter of his castle walls. He knew that such challenges were not to be trusted.

No-one knows who it was that killed the Sheriff. It happened at night, while he was walking round the camp, encouraging his men. An arrow aimed from the castle walls, struck him between the shoulder blades and passed clean through his heart, and when he fell his men took fright and one by one departed to their homes in Nottingham.

CHAPTER FOURTEEN

Richard the Lionheart

IN March 1194 King Richard returned from the Holy Land where he had won great glory. He had fought his way to within a few miles of Jerusalem, but the Saracens, under their brilliant leader Saladin, had been too good for him and had driven him back. Now he must return to England, to gather ships and men for a fresh attempt.

On his return, almost the first thing he heard was how the Sheriff of Nottingham had been done to death by a band of outlaws living wild in Sherwood Forest, led by a man named Robin Hood; and how they had been helped by Sir Richard of the Lea. So he decided to go and find out for himself what had really happened.

When he got to Nottingham with his bodyguard of soldiers and courtiers the story was so confused that he could make neither head nor tail of it. Some said that Robin was the wickedest man that ever drew a bow, that he was a thief and a murderer. Others that he was brave and noble, that he defended the weak against the strong, the poor against the rich and the godly against the ungodly.

'Tomorrow,' said the King, 'I shall take a troop of horsemen into the forest and capture this fellow. Then perhaps I shall get at the truth.'

'You will never capture Robin Hood except by stealth,' said the councillors who were looking after the city until they could choose a new Sheriff. 'If you take soldiers into the greenwood, the outlaws will melt away and you will be drawn deeper and deeper into the forest until you are lost. Then Robin and his men will pick you off one by one from their hiding places among the trees and rocks. They are swift and deadly archers and fear neither God nor man. The only way to meet him would be to go in the guise of a great abbot, accompanied by a troop of guards disguised as monks. You will surely then be captured and taken to the outlaws' hide-out. There you will meet their leader face to face.'

It was a dangerous proposal but Richard the Lionheart was used to danger. Indeed he enjoyed it. That was how he had got his famous name. So, bowing his head for the royal barber to shave a circle from its top, he followed his councillors' advice, laid aside his chainmail and his sword and gilded spurs and dressed himself in a rough woollen habit with its great cowl pulled well down to hide his red-gold hair and cast a shadow on his curling beard.

Then twenty of his finest men were told to dress themselves in the same way, but to wear their mailshirts and swords and daggers under their habits in case it came to a fight.

Lastly orders were given for the King's white surcoat, with the blood-red cross of the Crusaders on its front, to be carefully folded and laid at the bottom of a strong oak coffer together with his belt and cloak and spurs and glittering crown. Then a ledge was nailed all round the inside of the coffer and some thin boards cut to size and dropped down on to it, shutting the garments in a sort of secret cupboard. Lastly the top part of the coffer was filled with old threadbare habits and well-worn leather belts and some rolls of parchment and a broken crucifix, all mixed up together.

Next morning the party started out for the forest, some riding, some on foot. And suddenly, just as they had hoped, they were surrounded by a swarm of outlaws, all with bows bent and arrows laid upon the strings.

When asked where they were going and what was their business, the Abbot replied that they had been told of a famous outlaw named Robin Hood and that they wanted to meet him. They had heard many stories about him, some good and some bad. Now they wanted to find out the truth.

This was the first time anyone had ever come asking to meet Robin in this peaceful way. Usually they came hunting him, bent on killing him or bringing him to the gallows, but these people came unarmed and friendly. So after much whispering and discussion among themselves the outlaws agreed to lead the way to their secret hide-out.

At last, by many winding and confusing tracks, taking care that their guests should lose all sense of direction, they reached it; and there, sitting with Little John and Friar Tuck, was the man the Abbot had come to meet.

When he saw his guests approaching, Robin rose to greet them. 'Why do you trust your lives and limbs with outlaws?' he asked. 'Or did you have no choice?'

'We came to meet the famous Robin Hood,' replied the Abbot, 'to learn the truth about him, and about his men.'

'I am the man you seek,' said Robin, 'and these are my comrades. What do you wish to know?'

'Some swear you are good men and true,' said the Abbot.

'Others that you are traitors to your king. Some say you are skilled in weapons, especially with the bow; others that your fame is only hearsay, spread by yourselves to frighten travellers. We come to learn the truth.'

'What will convince you?' asked Robin, scornfully.

'A contest, man to man, with bow and broadsword,' said the Abbot.

'With you? With men of God?'

'Nay, not with us,' said the Abbot, smiling good-humouredly. 'Between yourselves. Show us your quality. Prove that you are the men you claim to be, that Robin Hood is more than a name to frighten children and make travellers tremble.'

'First let me see what you carry in your coffer,' said Robin. 'You may be richer than you look.'

'Only the trappings of the cloister,' said the Abbot, lifting the lid and scrabbling through its humble contents. He knew he was taking a great risk and that Robin might at any moment thrust his arm deep into the coffer and discover the false bottom. But he did it so naturally and openly that Robin immediately stopped him.

'Nay my Lord Abbot, I have eyes,' he said. 'I see you travel poorly, as the scriptures teach. I need to see no more.'

So the Abbot dropped the lid and the coffer was laid aside.

Now that they felt sure the Abbot and his party were really what they claimed to be, Robin and his men set up their targets and began to draw lots for who should shoot. Also which ones should fight with broadswords. And Robin three times split the wand and Little John split it twice. And many more put arrows close to the centre of the target from eighty yards away. Then Friar Tuck took on three of the strongest with his broadsword and beat them backwards, slashing like a madman till the forest rang with the sound of steel on steel.

'Now to make sure you are convinced,' said Robin. 'I have an outlaw wife who shoots and fights with the best of us. She too would like to show her quality.'

So Marian also shot, hitting the gold three times. Then took on Robin with her broadsword, giving him one of the hardest fights he had ever had.

'Now,' said Robin, 'Can we show you more?'

The Abbot's answer surprised everyone. 'Have you a wrestler?' he asked. 'In former days I tried that sport and was a fair performer. If one of you would care to match with me I will doff my godly habit and try a fall or two.'

'You shall try Little John,' said Robin, 'he is our wrestler,' and he winked at the men around him, certain that John would soon make the Abbot cry for mercy.

'Come lads, and make a ring!'

The outlaws gathered round in a rough circle and Little John began to strip to the waist in preparation for the match. The monks gathered round their Abbot while he also stripped, so that no-one saw the magnificent body which had all this while lain hidden beneath the rough habit.

But when his followers moved aside there stepped forth a giant, massive of shoulder and with mighty arms, with red-gold hair curling about the brow which until now had been hidden under his cowl. He was not as tall as John nor as broad, but the muscles rippled like steel cords under the smooth skin and he moved with cat-like ease.

At first the two men grappled warily, trying each other's strength. Then Little John began to force the Abbot backwards into the ring of monks and outlaws sitting and standing around, until at last he threw him down, pressing both his shoulders to the ground. Thus the first fall went to John.

But when the Abbot came out for the second round his strength seemed to have doubled and he soon had John groaning as he bent him backwards till his sinews cracked. John gritted his teeth and tried to twist his way out of the Abbot's iron grip. But all in vain. Inch by inch his shoulders were forced downwards until at last they touched the grass. So the second fall went to the Abbot.

Now came the third and last round and once more the Abbot

came out like a man refreshed, his strength re-doubled. For after circling round for a few moments he suddenly grasped Little John by the waist, lifted him bodily into the air and threw him over his shoulder into the cheering crowd. The Abbot was the winner by two falls to one.

In the ordinary way John would have taken little notice of such a tumble, he was so fit and strong. But this time he was unlucky. As he fell his head collided with Mark Tardiffe's, knocking them both senseless, and it was some little time before they sat up and began to wonder what had happened to them.

From the moment he saw the Abbot stripped for action, Robin had been suspicious. Now, as soon as he was satisfied that Little John and Mark were not badly hurt, he stepped forward and cried aloud to the smooth-skinned victor. 'You are no Abbot! You are some champion from afar sent here to prove your mettle. Tell us your name and title, whence you come and why.'

The Abbot had by this time rejoined his followers, as if to don his habit once again. But when their ranks divided and he stepped out from amongst them, he was wearing his white surcoat emblazoned with the crimson cross and round his waist his belt and broadsword. On his red-gold brow he wore a kingly crown studded with diamonds and rubies, and when he spoke his voice was proud and noble.

'I am King Richard, known as Lionheart.'

For a moment there was silence. Then, as the outlaws began to realise who the champion wrestler was, they gave a mighty shout.

'Long live King Richard, England's noble King.'

Then, led by Robin, they all bared their heads and knelt, and Tricket stole quietly forward and licked King Richard's foot as if she recognised true Majesty when she saw it.

Patting her on the head the King stepped forward, took Robin by the arm and raised him up. And all the outlaws stood and crowded round, laying their hands upon the royal shoulders, so that in after years they could tell their grandchildren that they had touched the greatest king in Christendom.

King Richard and his men spent all day with the outlaws, feasting and drinking, shooting with bow and arrow, fighting with broadsword and playing at quarterstaff; ending up with a melée in which he and twenty of his men fought a mock battle with Robin and twenty of his. The King was amazed at the outlaws' strength and skill. Indeed when it came to broadsword Friar Tuck beat the King himself, making him laughingly sue for mercy. But Little John and Mark had to sit on a tree-trunk watching the fun while the bumps on their heads grew bigger and bigger.

Meanwhile Sir Richard of the Lea and his lovely wife were sent for, and they all sat down to supper, the King facing Robin, with Sir Richard on his left hand and his lady on his right. And the King swore that it was many a year since he had tasted finer food or better cooked.

After supper, sitting round the camp fire, they told the King how they had become outlaws and how they had been forced to fight the Sheriff and his men and how, but for Sir Richard and his wife, many more of their company would have been caught and hanged.

They reminded the King that before the Normans came and the forest laws became so harsh, a man could keep his family fed without breaking the law, and the Church had been kinder and more loving, and the countryside had not been swarming with castles. Now there were thirty or forty in the north alone, which

was only just beginning to recover from the fearful attacks made by King William more than a hundred years before, when he brought his army into Yorkshire to punish the people for rebelling against him.

'What we need,' said Sir Richard of the Lea as the embers died down, 'is something that only your Majesty can grant. A Charter. With all our rights set down, what men may do and what they may not do, what land is private and what land is free.'

'A Book of Rules that all sides would obey,' said Robin.

'A mighty task,' replied the King.

''Twould be a mighty Charter!' said Robin.

'A Magna Charter,' said Friar Tuck always ready to show off his Latin. 'One day who knows, we might be known as Chartists!'

King Richard listened courteously. For four years he had been fighting in the Holy Land, so he knew nothing of the wrongs that were being done while he was away. He promised to look into all the outlaws' grievances and try to put things right.

And so, late in the evening, he and his bodyguard rode back into Nottingham and Robin and Sir Richard and his wife and all the outlaws rode with them like a guard of honour, with Tricket trotting along beside them. And in Nottingham they rested for the night.

Next morning Robin and his men paid homage to the King and swore to be faithful to him all their lives. And he gathered them back into the arms of the law where they had so long deserved to be. And in the same little church where Robin had fought his terrible battle with the Sheriff's guard all those months before, a Mass was said and the King knelt at the altar with Robin at his side, and as they took the bread and wine and thanked Jesus for having shed his blood for them, a great peace filled the air as if the Holy Spirit had come to give them a very special blessing.

Finally I must tell you how King Richard took a fancy to Tricket and how, when he finally set out for London, he took her with him, to be mated with Roland his favourite hound.

'I fear she is a mongrel,' said Robin.

'Yea, but with perfect manners,' said the King, 'for she lay at my feet all through supper time and never once sat up to beg a morsel from my plate! Besides,' he added, 'I lead a mongrel army, mixture of ancient British blood with Roman, Saxon, Norse and Norman, and could not wish for better.'

So Tricket was mated with Roland and had seven lovely puppies and King Richard kept three and sent Tricket back to the greenwood with the other four. And they were four of the most beautiful puppies ever born!

CHAPTER FIFTEEN

The Death of Robin

IN the end Robin died. He was only forty-seven years old but he had led a hard life in the Greenwood, always in danger, always watchful, always responsible for the safety of his men. Then, quite suddenly, he lost his beloved Marian. She was out in the forest gathering herbs one stormy autumn evening, accompanied by the faithful Tricket, when a great bough, torn by the howling wind from the trunk of an ancient oak tree, fell and crushed her.

She heard the rending sound and could have saved herself, but as she ran forward to drag Tricket clear, the bough swung sideways through the air and caught her across the spine, killing her instantly and pinning her to the forest floor. Poor Tricket stood beside her for an hour or more, whining and licking her face, but she made no movement and soon her body was cold. So the faithful hound raced back to the camp, barking like a mad thing, begging Robin and Little John to follow her, clawing at their boots, then running on ahead once more, then returning to claw at them again, until they followed her into the forest.

At last they reached the spot where poor Marian lay. Lifting the bough clear, they carried her dear body gently back into the camp, dressed her in her wedding dress and filled her hair with flowers, then laid her in the earth. And they all wept as Friar Tuck spoke the burial words.

From then onwards, Robin was never the same. It was as if half his life had been torn away. At last he fell sick of a fever and was so ill that he could scarcely stand.

'We must get him to Kirklees,' said Friar Tuck. 'The Abbess there is skilled with herbs and healing balms. Some years ago she cured the cellarer of Fountains when he was close to death.'

So they made a simple stretcher covered with deer skin and padded with fern and bracken, and a small party led by Will Scarlet and Alan a'Dale set off to carry Robin northwards, taking it in turns to bear their precious burden two by two, while their comrades moved ahead with arrows already laid on their bow-strings, in case they should be ambushed on the way.

Three days they walked, carrying by day and sheltering by night. And at last there was the Abbey lying in the valley, with woodlands riding up the hillsides all around.

The Abbess received them courteously and had Robin put into a bedroom opening upon the sunrise, and one of her nuns brought rosewater and moistened his lips and cooled his fevered brow. 'Now at last,' thought Little John, 'he will get well and we shall soon be home again.'

But then there befell a strange and terrible chance. When the Abbess asked Little John his master's name, John answered, 'Robert Hood, a native of the moors near Pickering.' But as she went out of the room she heard him call Robin by his outlaw name, not 'Robert Hood' but 'Robin'. Then she knew he must be the leader of the outlaw band well known in Sherwood, who murdered the monk on his way to London bearing the Sheriff's letter to Prince John. That monk had been her brother.

So now, although she fought hard against it, the Abbess had only one thought, to be revenged. It was unchristian, it was unholy. The fifth Commandment said, 'Thou shalt not kill.' But she remembered some other words in the Bible which spoke of 'An eye for an eye and a tooth for a tooth,' and she could not get them out of her mind. All night she prayed, asking God to guide her. But always her brother's bloodstained head kept appearing to her, whispering 'Kill him! Kill him!' until in the end she was helpless. Fate had put her brother's murderer into her power and she could not resist. Robin Hood must die. He had deserved no less.

Soon after dawn she stole quietly into Robin's room with knife and cupping bowl.

'To kill the fever you must first be bled,' she said caressingly, and taking his right arm she cut the artery just inside the elbow where it bends, then left him there to bleed. It was only a tiny cut and Robin hardly noticed it, but his heart began to pump out his life's blood in a small but steady stream, and soon he was so weak that he fainted. And still the tiny stream of blood flowed on.

Later in the morning when Little John came to see how he had slept, Robin was only just alive. His bed was stained deep red and he was so weak and pale he could hardly sit up. Little John pressed his finger to the wound and stopped the bleeding. But it was too late. Robin had little more blood to give. He was already close to death.

When the Abbess returned, Little John turned to her in fury. 'A thousand curses on you, wretched woman,' he said. 'You have killed the greatest man in England.'

'He, to his everlasting shame,' hissed the Abbess, 'was a party

to killing my dear brother, a monk of Nottingham, as he rode by Sherwood with letters for Prince John. You brought him to be cured and I have cured him. All ills are cured by death.' And she laughed an evil laugh as she swept out of the room.

Now Little John realised that he and Will and Alan and the others were all in deadly danger. This woman would stop at nothing to have them captured and killed. They must leave the Abbey at once. And Robin agreed. 'No point in risking all our lives,' he whispered. 'One death is more than enough. Go, tell them to be gone without delay.'

Swiftly John made his way to the dormitory where Will and Alan and the others had been quartered. He told them what had happened and gave them Robin's orders. They must leave Kirklees at once. They must melt away into the forest, leaving him to guard Robin till the last moment, then fend for himself. Within a few minutes the dormitory was clear and they were gone, striking southwards back to Sherwood, while John returned to Robin.

When he entered the sick room, Robin lay pale and listless, his eyes large and shining, as if he were already gazing into Eternity. 'My end is near. I would shoot one arrow more before I die. Give me my bow and throw the window wide.'

Little John strung Robin's bow and placed it in his hands, then laid an arrow on the string. Then he opened the window and lifted Robin up in bed, supporting him with his strong right arm. As he felt the bow, all Robin's strength seemed to return, and he smiled as he pushed it forward from the string. The arrow flew through the window and soared over the lake into the trees beyond, a good two hundred yards.

Then looking up into John's eyes, Robin whispered, 'Bury me where the arrow fell and tell no man the place. Tell them in

Sherwood that I love them and that my spirit will hover over them for all eternity. Farewell.' Then, falling back into John's arms, he died.

Blinded with tears, Little John lowered Robin's body on to the bed, then knelt and prayed that Jesus would receive his soul in Heaven and keep it safe. Then he lifted him up and carried him out into the woods, laying his body on a flowered bank while he went in search of the arrow.

At last he found it, fastened to a giant sycamore, deep in the woods beside the Abbey millstream. Now he must find a spade to dig the grave.

Marking the tree which the arrow had pierced, John made his way out of the woods into the open and there, close at hand, was a simple hut where dwelt the woodman who cut logs for the Abbey fires, and timber to repair its roof. 'There surely,' said he, 'I shall find a spade.'

Stealing carefully forwards he entered the little lean-to at the back of the hut and there, among the woodman's tools, he found a trenching iron with which to carve a shallow grave.

When the grave was ready John took Robin's body in his arms and carried it to the grave like a mother carrying her sleeping child. Then went down on his knees and laid it in its last resting place, covering it with turf and leaves. Then knelt and said a prayer, asking Jesus and his Mother to take Robin's soul into their keeping.

Finally he returned to the woodman's hut and put back the spade, then began to tramp the long road back to Sherwood. He alone had found the arrow. He alone had dug the grave. He alone knew where Robin was buried. And with him the secret died.

That is why to this very day no-one knows where Robin's body lies.

In any case, it was only his body that died. In Sherwood his spirit lived on and the fame of his bowmen spread throughout the land. Indeed, for another two hundred years and more, men came to Sherwood to be trained to use the bow. When they enlisted they would boast, 'I am Sherwood trained. I shoot like Robin Hood.' And kings were proud to have them in their ranks they were such mighty bowmen.

But Robin Hood stands for more than that. He was one of the first in a long line of men and women who believed that freedom is more precious than life itself. After centuries of struggle, that freedom has been handed down to you and me. It has been a long and up-hill battle, but for us and for our children it is won. Now we have the task of guarding it and of bringing it to others. And if Robin were alive today he would be among the first to help us.

That is why his name lives on and that is why it will never die.

Epilogue

SIX hundred years later, in the 1820's, somewhere near Bolsover – and no-one now remembers where, it was so long ago – two pitmen were hard at work sinking a shaft for a new coalmine. Suddenly the earth at the side of the shaft gave way and fell outwards in a yawning gap, and there in front of them was Robin's cave just as it was when he and his outlaws lived there all those years ago and just as they had left it. There was the fireplace full of wood ash and half-charred logs, with the iron pot and tripod in position. There were the blacksmith's and the bowyer's shops, the kitchen full of pots and pans, the sick bay with its herbs and bandages and splints, the storeroom full of sacks and barrels with salt and beans still in them. And against one wall a rack of bows and belts and broadswords, and quivers full of arrows. And at the end of one of the galleries the tiny chapel with the cross still on the altar. And the stream that had poured through the cave for thousands of year still bubbling along.

The two pitmen walked through the opening and stood staring like men in a dream. What was it they had found and where had it come from? At last they saw a skeleton wrapped in an old woollen habit, lying at the foot of a flat piece of wall, one hand holding a crucifix, the other a chisel. Looking up they saw a long list of names roughly scratched on the cavern wall. At the top of the list were the words 'These died that we might live. Requiescant in pace,' and at the bottom, painfully scored, 'I was the last, Michael Tuck.'

Yes, the skeleton was Friar Tuck's. He had just managed to crawl there and scratch these few words before he collapsed and died.

The two pitmen were now very nervous. It was all so weird. Their hearts pounded. They had the feeling that they had crossed some barrier that they had no right to cross, that

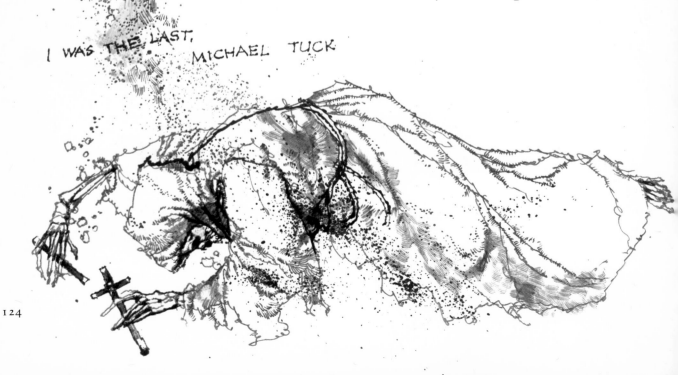

I WAS THE LAST, MICHAEL TUCK

they were in the presence of a great mystery. But one thing they were certain of. They must run and tell the nearest clergyman or schoolmaster and bring them here to see it. They would be able to explain.

But as they climbed the length of shaft they had cut, the stone began to break away under their feet and they had barely reached the top when there came a great rockfall from above, thundering downwards, filling the shaft and piling huge blocks high around it, some of the smaller ones only just missing them as they ran, and rattling around them like hail.

And when they got to the top and looked back, there was nothing to be seen but great blocks of stone settling into place, and a cloud of fine dust rising from the hillside. Everything that had been there before was buried; the opening they had cut, their ladder, their picks and shovels, their hammers and wedges and crowbars, the timbers for strengthening the shaft, all were buried under hundreds of tons of rock.

So when they told their story in the village no-one would believe them. People had heard the rocks rumbling downwards and had seen the cloud of dust rising from the hillside. But that sort of thing often happened and they only laughed when the pitmen tried to describe what they had seen.

Soon they themselves began to wonder whether the cave was really there or whether it had not been a sort of bewitching, brought on by the strong ale they had drunk with their dinner. And at last they forgot about it themselves and in time they both died and the secret was lost.

But what they had seen was truly Robin's cave, just as he and the outlaws had left it, and the two pitmen were the last ever to see it. But it is still there, only a little way below the ground close to one of the worked-out pits. And one fine day it will be found again. I wonder who will find it!

125

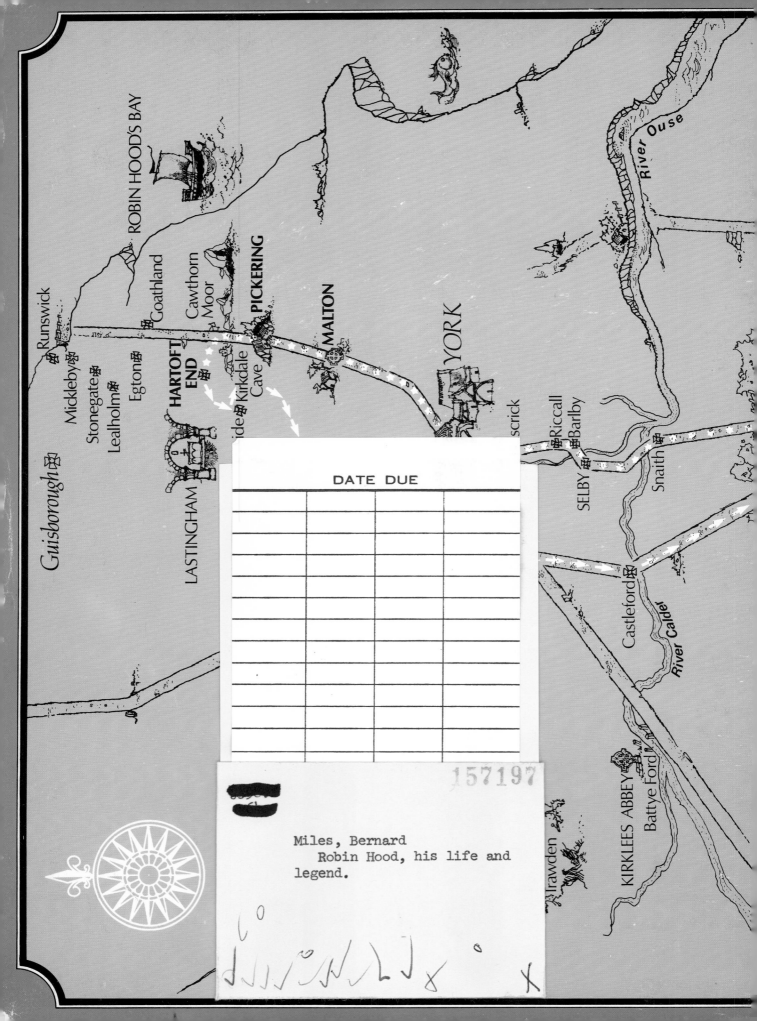